MW00388627

Raising Up
SPIRITUAL
CHAMPIONS

How to Teach Children to Think and Act Like Jesus

A DISCIPLESHIP COURSE FOR AGES 9 TO 12

HOW TO MAKE CLEAN COPIES FROM THIS BOOK

You may make copies of portions of this book with a clean conscience if

- you (or someone in your organization) are the original purchaser;

- you are using the copies you make for a noncommercial purpose (such as teaching or promoting your ministry) within your church or organization;

- you follow the instructions provided in this book.

However, it is ILLEGAL for you to make copies if

- you are using the material to promote, advertise or sell a product or service other than for ministry fund-raising;

- you are using the material in or on a product for sale; or

- you or your organization are not the original purchaser of this book.

By following these guidelines you help us keep our products affordable.

Thank you,

Gospel Light

Permission to make photocopies of or to reproduce by any other mechanical or electronic means in whole or in part any designated* page, illustration or activity in this book is granted only to the original purchaser and is intended for non-commercial use within a church or other Christian organization. None of the material in this book may be reproduced for any commercial promotion, advertising or sale of a product or service. Sharing of the material in this book with other churches or organizations not owned or controlled by the original purchaser is also prohibited. All rights reserved.

*Pages with the following notation can be legally reproduced:

© 2004 Gospel Light. Permission to photocopy granted. *Raising Up Spiritual Champions*

NOTE

Because church liability laws are inherently complex and may not be completely free of doubtful interpretations, you are advised to verify that the legal rules you are following actually apply to your situation. In no event will Gospel Light be liable for direct, indirect, special, incidental or consequential damages arising out of the use, inability to use or inappropriate use of the text materials, forms or documentation, even if Gospel Light is advised of or aware of the possibility of such damages. In no case will Gospel Light's liability exceed the amount of the purchase price paid.

Gospel Light in no way guarantees or warrants any particular legal or other result from the use of *Raising Up Spiritual Champions*.

While Gospel Light attempts to provide accurate and authoritative information regarding the subject matter covered, *Raising Up Spiritual Champions* is sold with the understanding that Gospel Light is not engaged in rendering legal or other professional services, and is sold subject to the foregoing limited warranty. If legal or other expert assistance is required, the services of a competent professional person should be sought.

Forms are shown for illustrative purposes only. They should not be relied on for any legal purpose or effect until they have been reviewed by a competent attorney in your state who is experienced in laws relating to churches.

Editorial Staff

Founder, Dr. Henrietta Mears • **Publisher Emeritus,** William T. Greig • **Publisher, Children's Curriculum and Resources,** Bill Greig III • **Senior Consulting Publisher,** Dr. Elmer L. Towns • **Product Line Manager,** Cary Maxon • **Senior Managing Editor,** Sheryl Haystead • **Senior Consulting Editor,** Wesley Haystead, M.S.Ed. • **Senior Editor, Biblical and Theological Issues,** Bayard Taylor, M.Div. • **Editorial Team,** Mary Davis, Lynnette Pennings • **Contributing Editors,** Debbie Barber, Ninalu Bovensiep, Sherry Ehrhart, Kevin Gordon, Rachel Hong, Diane Pitman • **Art Directors,** Lenndy McCullough, Christina Renée Sharp, Samantha A. Hsu • **Designer,** Zelle Olson

Scripture quotations are taken from the *Holy Bible, New International Version®.*

Copyright © 1973, 1978, 1984 by International Bible Society. Used by permission of Zondervan Publishing House. All rights reserved.

© 2004 Gospel Light, Ventura, CA 93006. All rights reserved. Printed in the U.S.A.

How to Use This Guide

If you are the children's pastor,

1. Read "Course Overview" on page 10 to get an understanding of the purpose and goals of **Raising Up Spiritual Champions**.

2. Using the job description on page 17, recruit a coordinator for **Raising Up Spiritual Champions**. Provide him or her with this book, including the two CDs.

3. Plan regular check-ins with the coordinator and be available for practical support and encouragement.

If you are the coordinator for **Raising Up Spiritual Champions**,

1. Read the articles in the Coordinator Information section that begins on page 9.

2. Use the Step-by-Step Planning Calendar on page 15 as your planning guide. (Tip: The calendar is on the CD-ROM found at the front of this book. Modify it to fit your church and print it out!)

If you are a teacher (called a "coach") for **Raising Up Spiritual Champions**,

1. Read "Course Overview" on page 10 to get an understanding of the purpose and goals of **Raising Up Spiritual Champions**.

2. Read "Get Ready to Coach!" on page 35.

3. Photocopy the materials you need for each session (see the Supply List on p. 213).

© 2004 Gospel Light. Permission to photocopy granted. *Raising Up Spiritual Champions*

Contents

Foreword

I recently had the privilege of having lunch with a world-renowned researcher. We were having an invigorating discussion about the state of the world and how people make life choices when I innocently noted that life is nothing more than an exercise in spiritual war, and every person chooses one side (i.e., God's) or the other (i.e., Satan's) in that war. Upon hearing this statement, my colleague leaned back in his chair, opened his eyes wide and guffawed in disbelief.

"You don't really believe that, do you?" he challenged me. "Do you honestly see the world in such simplistic, black-and-white terms?"

Here was a brilliant young man who had earlier described how he had been "raised in the Church" and had given evidence of some knowledge of scriptural passages. Yet, as we sought to agree upon the fundamental problems facing our nation today, he unwittingly exemplified what may be the most significant crisis of all: the absence of a biblical worldview in the minds and hearts of people. Like every human being, he had a worldview, but it was not a way of understanding and responding to life that reflected God's perspectives.

I am deeply concerned about the future of the Church and our society. Young people face a world that challenges them when they dare to acknowledge, understand, honor and serve God. Sadly, even most churches and Christian families do little to arm children for the battle in which they are immersed. Essentially, we send our children to war without the most basic tools required for survival, much less victory. One of the most important tools is having a biblical worldview—a mental, emotional and spiritual filter that enables you to interpret life from God's point of view.

How serious is this situation? Our national research studies indicate that if a child has not been exposed to such teaching and experiences before age 13, the chance of him or her developing such a life perspective is slim, at best. In fact, only 9 percent of all born-again adults in the United States currently possess a biblical worldview. Less than 3 percent of born-again teenagers have such a worldview.[1]

You may be surprised by these numbers. "How can that be?" many people have asked me. "We teach the Bible in our Christian education classes, and we preach the Bible from our pulpit. It's doubtful that we have that problem in my church." In actuality, though, we have found very few churches in which even half of the congregation possesses a biblical worldview; in fact, only half of all Protestant senior pastors have one![2] Good intentions, numerous programs and well-attended services and events rarely correlate with a congregation in which a substantial number of individuals have a biblical worldview.

Why are the numbers of Christians with a biblical worldview so small? Because in most churches—and in most Christian families—there has not been a deliberate, systematic attempt to teach young people how to think like Jesus. Shaping the thinking process is a vital starting point because you cannot *act* like Jesus until you can *think* like Him. Simply knowing the Bible characters and a few dozen Bible tales and regurgitating some Bible verses isn't good enough. You have to understand the mind of God and the nature of life before you have the capacity to imitate the life of Christ.

Worldview development can happen either by intent or default. For most Americans, it is worldview by default, as they naively embrace the unfortunate points-of-view pressed upon them by movies, television, music, school texts and the like. Alternatively, we can take the charge of Deuteronomy 6:1-9 seriously, seizing the learning moments to which we have access and preparing our children for a life of obedience, love, service and wisdom. Just as our children's worldview is crafted either by default or intent, so is our shepherding of that process conducted in ignorance or intelligence.

Will you accept the challenge to help shape the minds and hearts of young people? Remember, research convincingly demonstrates that we cannot afford to wait until the teen years, much less the college or adult years, to instigate this process. The moral convictions, spiritual choices and core theological beliefs of most people are solidified before they reach age 13.[3]

That's where curriculum comes into the picture. I am excited that Gospel Light understands this urgent need to help young people develop a worldview based upon God's principles. The curriculum you hold in your hands has been designed to assist you in empowering children to think like Jesus so that they can act like Jesus. By helping them to grasp the answers to basic questions regarding the existence and nature of God, the purpose of life, the significance of creation, the fundamental realities regarding truth, spiritual authority and salvation, young people can navigate through the churning waters of a culture seemingly bent on its own destruction.[4] Every parent and ministry leader not only owes such training to children, but also will someday be held accountable for how well he or she provided such preparation for life. Use this curriculum as one tool that will enable you to raise children in the ways they should go in order to honor God and to make the most of the precious life He has given them.

George Barna
Ventura, California
October 2004

Notes

1. George Barna, *Think Like Jesus* (Nashville, TN: Integrity Books, 2003), pp. 19-24.
2. George Barna, "Only Half of Protestant Pastors Have a Biblical Worldview," *The Barna Update*, January 12, 2004. http://www.barna.org (accessed October 2004).
3. George Barna, *Transforming Children into Spiritual Champions* (Ventura, CA: Regal Books, 2003), pp. 32-41.
4. George Barna, *Think Like Jesus*, pp. 48-51.

Coordinator Information

This section contains concise and practical information that can help you plan and lead the **Raising Up Spiritual Champions** program. Included in this section are an overview of how this program works, a planning calendar, guidelines for recruiting and training volunteers, publicity suggestions, as well as decorating ideas and helpful tips for follow-up after the program ends.

Course Overview

Welcome to **Raising Up Spiritual Champions,** an intensive discipleship course for children ages 9-12, their families and their churches. With its sports theme, games and interactive studies, **Raising Up Spiritual Champions** is a winning combination for helping young believers understand the basics of growing in a relationship with Jesus Christ and His Body, the Church.

WHO? The Team Members, Parents, Mentors, Coaches

Raising Up Spiritual Champions is designed for children ages 9-12. It assumes that the child (called a team member throughout the course) has made a personal commitment to Christ and has indicated an interest in learning about being a disciple of Jesus.

It also assumes that there will be a level of parent participation, primarily with *Student Page* assignments to be completed at home. Each *Student Page* contains a Family Challenge as well as other activities for which a parent signs off when the activity is completed. During the Practice segment of each session, team members check in with their teachers to record completed activities. In addition, a *Parent Page* is sent home after each session. *Parent Pages* focus on ways parents can support their children in ongoing discipleship at home. Families are also invited to be part of the celebration in Session 8. If a child does not have family members who are able or interested in participating, recruit several mature Christians in your church to serve as mentors for one or more children.

These mentors should be willing to meet with the children during the week, help complete the at-home activities and participate in the Session 8 celebration.

The teachers for this course are designated as coaches throughout. They need neither to be sports-minded nor physical fitness buffs! The paradigm of a sports team is used not to exclude those who aren't sports players but rather to emphasize that God's team has no second-string players. It includes all kinds of people!

© 2004 Gospel Light. Permission to photocopy granted. *Raising Up Spiritual Champions*

WHY? The Purpose and Goals

The purpose of *Raising Up Spiritual Champions* is to give young members of God's family a solid foundation for healthy growth into whole-hearted followers of Jesus Christ.

Young believers sometimes learn behaviors or habits without understanding the biblical groundwork for them. **Raising Up Spiritual Champions** seeks first to help students understand from the Bible why followers of Jesus think, feel and act the way they do! This is done through Bible study, Bible skills development and a variety of interactive teaching methods that will get kids thinking and talking as they open God's Word for themselves!

The second goal is to help young believers understand how God's Word relates to their lives and practice specific ways to put God's Word into action. The Practice portion of each lesson links to the *Student Page* in such a way that every team member goes home with information discovered and discussed in class. This information helps students get started on what they will do at home during the week. The team member and his or her family will be encouraged to get involved in these application activities. The activities provide an additional way for parents to sharpen their skills as the primary disciple makers of their children.

The third goal is to foster relationships within the church, building a community in which young believers are lovingly mentored beyond the duration of this course. According to the Bible, spiritual community centered on Jesus Christ is the most powerful bond

there is! To foster our third goal of building community, **Raising Up Spiritual Champions** contains many opportunities for leaders and teachers to freely share what God is doing in their own lives. These examples powerfully build community as younger believers learn from others' experiences.

Another way to accomplish the third goal of community is the use of sports themes and terminology. Though people may not always understand "community," they generally do understand the concept of a sports team! No matter if a team wins or loses, it is commonly understood that a team works together to achieve a goal. A team shares victories and defeats. More experienced players help rookies gain needed skills not only to improve rookies' lives but also because the better each one becomes, the stronger the entire team grows. It's truly a win-win situation that we understand and can apply to the Body of Christ!

This course is designed to help you build a team of both rookies and seasoned vets that will bring lifelong blessing and victory to individual believers, to our churches and to the entire Body of Christ—the ultimate team!

© 2004 Gospel Light. Permission to photocopy granted. *Raising Up Spiritual Champions*

For a 60-Minute Session

Warm-Up 10 minutes

Power-Up 20 minutes

Practice 20 minutes

Rally 10 minutes

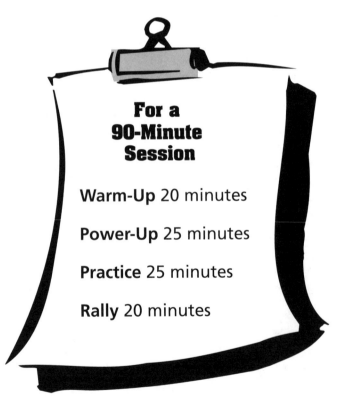

For a 90-Minute Session

Warm-Up 20 minutes

Power-Up 25 minutes

Practice 25 minutes

Rally 20 minutes

WHAT? The Schedule

The **Raising Up Spiritual Champions** intensive discipleship course consists of eight sessions. The first six are teaching sessions. The seventh session is a review and planning session. The eighth session is designated as an evaluation and celebration that involves families while reinforcing the learning that has taken place.

Session Format

The teaching sessions in **Raising Up Spiritual Champions** consist of four time segments: Warm-Up, Power-Up, Practice and Rally. Coaches lead students (called team members) in a variety of activities. There should be one coach for each group (or team) of 8 to 12 team members. Assistants (called trainers) may also be present.

Warm-Up (10-20 minutes) is a time for team members in groups of 8 to 12 to have fun while preparing their minds for learning. The time includes games and brainstorming activities designed to introduce the session topic and help team members express what they already know about the topic.

Power-Up (20-30 minutes) presents to team members in groups of 8 to 12 a scriptural concept related to following Jesus through Bible studies, skits, discussion questions and other group interaction.

Practice (20-30 minutes) helps team members in groups of 8 to 12 apply and personalize the information discovered in Power-Up through a variety of games and activities. Each team member begins work on his or her *Student Page* in this time segment. After the first week, team members check in with their coaches during Practice to record completed at-home activities from the previous session's *Student Page*.

Rally (10-20 minutes) is an all-group gathering time featuring worship songs and prayer as well as optional team-building activities. This worship time may be led by a coach or the **Raising Up Spiritual Champions** coordinator. (Optional: Team members may meet with their coaches to pray in small groups.) Each team member leaves Rally time with his or her *Student Page* and a *Parent Page*.

© 2004 Gospel Light. Permission to photocopy granted. *Raising Up Spiritual Champions*

Sessions 7 and 8 vary slightly. Session 7 contains a review activity during the Power-Up time and uses the brainstorming posters made in Sessions 1-6. In Session 7, team members are also given the opportunity to create a personal discipleship plan and creative reminder. During Session 8, the coach leads all team members, parents and assistants together in celebration, award and commitment activities during the Power-Up, Practice and Rally time segments. (In a large program, all team members, coaches and trainers gather together. A coach, the **Raising Up Spiritual Champions** coordinator or the children's pastor may lead the activities.)

Because of the open-ended nature of some activities, it is recommended that each session should be at least an hour. You may extend the time for each session by adding a snack and/or outdoor recreation time.

Customize Sessions for Your Group

As you prepare for a session, note the skills needed and the level of understanding required. Take an extra five minutes to look at your class roster and think about how best to adapt specific activities to your particular group's needs. For instance, a group of poor readers would enjoy hearing a skit read aloud to them by adults, while a group containing good readers who enjoy reading aloud would probably rather perform the skit themselves. The same principle applies to other activities. For instance, if some in your group do not like to write, include drawing as an option for answering questions or invite team members to dictate responses to their coaches. Adapt games as needed to fit your facility and to ensure that all children can be successful participants.

The goal of adaptation is to form a genuine team atmosphere in which everyone is loved and respected!

No one should feel penalized, but rather, everyone should feel that he or she is being helped to learn as much as possible. This kind of adaptation is one way we as adults model the Christlike attitudes and actions we want children to learn and show. Teaching children how to be disciples of Jesus Christ is far more effective when the adults "walk the talk" than when we simply talk at children about what they are supposed to do! This simple adaptation process is one way we effectively build community in Christ. We're sending this message to the children: You are important. We all help each other. We can learn better together. All of us—rookies, veterans, coaches, parents—are on the same team.

WHEN? The Time Frame

This course might be taught in a variety of situations:

● As part of a retreat or camp program

● As a rite-of-passage focus or preparatory program for students about to move into middle or junior high school (replacing temporarily a Sunday or weeknight program)

● As a summer program of one day or evening per week (Saturday afternoon, Wednesday night, etc.) over eight weeks' time

● As part of a home-school study program

● As part of a Christian school curriculum, perhaps to end the year's Bible class

● As a summer Sunday School or Bible club program for selected students

● As a supplement to denominational confirmation classes

© 2004 Gospel Light. Permission to photocopy granted. *Raising Up Spiritual Champions*

WHERE? The Space

Raising Up Spiritual Champions can be customized to fit nearly any space. Because of its sports theme, it might be desirable to have part of the program outdoors, weather permitting. Some games include an outdoor option. If you are extending the session time through the use of recreational games and snack time, the outdoor options are especially helpful.

You might ask, "Why have games at all? Isn't this a serious discipleship course?" Indeed it is serious business! And one way we can show how serious we are about this is to present the information in ways that have been proven effective. Incorporating movement and social interaction are two effective ways to help people think better, learn more and retain information longer! Of course, these are also the basic components of a simple game! Children (and adults) do some of their best thinking while they are in motion. So if we're already presenting the material, why not make the effort to teach it as effectively as possible?

Indoor space of any kind can be used—classrooms, gymnasiums, fellowship halls. Ample space is needed for team members to congregate during Rally time; wall space should be available to place and add to brainstorming posters (preferably kept on walls and added to from week to week). Clear an open area in the room for games to be played. If indoor space is too small, consider using a park or playground for

part of the session. Or, adapt the games to be played around a table or in a small amount of space.

Indoor space should be decorated to reflect the theme. For specific ideas, refer to "Room Decorations" on page 22.

HOW? The Materials

Raising Up Spiritual Champions doesn't require unusual materials. Common classroom supplies are needed: pencils, markers, paper, large sheets of construction paper, butcher paper, poster board and masking tape are frequently used. Session-related pages (Resource Pages such as skits, game cards, etc., and *Student Pages* and *Parent Pages*) can be printed directly from the CD-ROM in the front of this book or photocopied from this book (see contents). Session-related pages are found immediately following each session.

Materials for other activities are usually common household or classroom items, making it easy to gather items and prepare for each session. Read through the Session Game Plan at least a week ahead of time to make gathering of all materials easy! Refer to the Supply List on page 213 for an easy-to-use list of all supplies needed. (Note: Unless otherwise specified, supplies are listed for a team of 8 to 12 students. For larger groups, collect duplicate sets of materials.)

© 2004 Gospel Light. Permission to photocopy granted. *Raising Up Spiritual Champions*

Step-by-Step Planning Calendar

Personalize and adapt this calendar according to your own church's needs.
Your support staff can execute many of the items on this list.

16 WEEKS BEFORE

- Pray, asking for God's help and guidance as you plan and organize.
- Determine time, format, learning plan and location.
- Check with appropriate church personnel about availability of location.
- Set dates in conjunction with all-church calendar.
- Recruit an assistant director and an event/publicity coordinator.

12 WEEKS BEFORE

- Meet with assistant director and event/publicity coordinator:
    1. Pray.
    2. Review and finalize session schedule.
    3. Set deadline dates for all preparations.
    4. List all staff needs.
    5. Compile lists of prospective coaches (teachers) and trainers (assistants or small-group leaders). (In larger churches, recruit a head coach as well.) Determine who will contact each prospect and set a deadline for all recruiting to be completed.
    6. Set date for training meeting(s).
    7. Plan publicity.
- Event/publicity coordinator customizes a personnel recruitment flyer (see p. 197) and student publicity flyer (see p. 198) for the church bulletin or newsletter (see p. 197).

10 WEEKS BEFORE

- Confirm preliminary assignments with coaches and trainers, notifying recruits of training meeting date(s). Identify any new staff additions and remaining vacancies. Make plans for additional recruiting as needed.
- Meet with assistant director and event/publicity coordinator:
    1. Pray.
    2. Plan training meeting(s) and assign responsibilities.
    3. Plan Session 8 Family Celebration.
- Choose and make arrangements for one or two service projects team members may complete (see Session 6 *Student Page*).

8 WEEKS BEFORE

- Announce training meeting(s).
- Make bulletin or newsletter insert listing activity supplies, refreshments and other materials needed.
- Photocopy and prepare all curriculum materials. Make a copy of the *Champions Music* CD for each team member, coach and trainer.
- Register team members.

4 WEEKS BEFORE

- Distribute curriculum materials to coaches and trainers.
- Conduct training meeting(s):
    1. Present overview of course content.
    2. Sing songs from the *Champions Music* CD and distribute copies of this CD.
    3. Explain time schedule and responsibilities of coaches and trainers.
    4. Have coaches and trainers meet together to make lesson and activity plans.
    5. Pray together.

© 2004 Gospel Light. Permission to photocopy granted. *Raising Up Spiritual Champions*

Recruit and Train Coaches

Recruiting Guidelines

Recruiting is one of your most important duties as coordinator. To build a strong crew of coaches and trainers, keep the following guidelines in mind:

● Start early (see the Step-by-Step Planning Calendar on p. 15).

● Pray for guidance in finding the right people to serve in this ministry.

● Be sure you have a clear job description for each position to be filled (see "Job Descriptions" below and on pp. 17-18, and adapt as needed).

● Create a list of prospects. Don't forget youth, parents, college students and senior citizens! Plan for one coach and one trainer (adult or teen) for each group of 8 to 12 team members.

● Share further recruiting responsibilities with the leaders you recruit first.

● Regularly present information to the congregation about the **Raising Up Spiritual Champions** program. Distribute volunteer recruitment flyers in personal mailings to your prospect list.

● Personally contact each prospect. Challenge each one with the importance of this ministry. Explain the training and resources you will offer to help the prospect succeed. If you must recruit a large number of people, schedule meetings with groups of prospects.

● Allow each prospect time to pray about the opportunity. Resist the temptation to arm-twist; you don't want volunteers who are not truly interested and committed!

● Screen all potential staff. Use your church's forms and policies to select responsible volunteers.

RECRUITING A REFEREE

Just for fun, recruit a volunteer to be the "referee" during sessions. This volunteer wears a referee's shirt, keeps time, signals transitions (with or without blowing a whistle), participates in activities alongside team members who need help staying focused and helps as needed.

© 2004 Gospel Light. Permission to photocopy granted. *Raising Up Spiritual Champions*

Job Descriptions

Coordinator

- Schedules **Raising Up Spiritual Champions** program, coordinating dates, times and facilities with the overall church calendar and other church staff as needed

- Recruits, trains and oversees volunteers by providing materials and facilitating communication within the program

Coach

- Prepares and then leads a group of 8 to 12 team members to participate in each session's activities

- Builds relationships with each team member during the **Raising Up Spiritual Champions** program

- Plans and leads one or more follow-up group activities with team members

Trainer

- Assists coaches with their responsibilities

- Builds relationships with each team member during the **Raising Up Spiritual Champions** program

- Participates in one or more follow-up group activities with team members

Secretary/Registrar

- Registers team members and maintains attendance records
- Communicates number of registrations to curriculum expert
- Prepares team rosters for coaches and trainers
- Provides team members' contact information as needed to publicity/event coordinator

Publicity/Event Coordinator

- Plans and carries out publicity to recruit coaches and trainers
- Plans and carries out publicity to encourage team member participation in the **Raising Up Spiritual Champions** program
- Plans and carries out publicity to team members and families for the Session 8 Family Celebration

Curriculum Expert

- Prepares curriculum materials for each session (Sessions, Resource Pages, *Student Pages*, *Parent Pages*), printing out materials from the CD-ROM or making photocopies from this book
- Optional: Collects binders for *Student Page* Playbooks (see Session 1)

Team Manager

- Prepares the location where sessions take place by setting up room(s) and needed equipment
- Places materials for each activity where they are needed

© 2004 Gospel Light. Permission to photocopy granted. *Raising Up Spiritual Champions*

Training Overview

Invite all coaches, trainers and other volunteers to meet together at least a month before the **Raising Up Spiritual Champions** program begins. It is important for your staff to meet together, not only to receive the essential information they need to know, but also to receive spiritual, emotional and practical support from each other. Follow the tips below to plan an effective meeting.

Tip 1: Plan Your Agenda

There are two types of training information you need to communicate to coaches, trainers and other volunteers. In addition, provide some time for fellowship. Start the meeting with an icebreaker game (play Charades and have volunteers act out sports equipment or the names of famous athletes for others to guess) to help your volunteers get to know each other and build friendships and to foster team unity.

Basic Information

● Introduction to the **Raising Up Spiritual Champions** program. Briefly describe the goals, overview and outline of the course, etc.).

● General information. Summarize essential dates, session schedule, location(s), procedures, supplies, etc.

Skill Training

● Job descriptions. Give a brief overview of each job and provide written job descriptions to each volunteer.

● Topics that volunteers need most to be effective in working with team members. Choose one or two of the articles on pages 27-50 to copy and distribute to your volunteers. (Recommended articles: "Get Ready to Coach!" and "Benefits of Building Relationships.") Additional articles may be distributed and discussed as needed during the program in response to a particular need or a volunteer's request.

Tip 2: Prepare for the Meeting

● Schedule each meeting at a time you think most volunteers will be able to attend. Many churches schedule meetings on Saturday morning or Sunday after church. Provide child care if needed. Reserve your chosen date on the church calendar.

● As you recruit, make sure you let all volunteers know the date of your meeting—either in person, by phone, by mail or by e-mail. Publicize each meeting in your church bulletin. Mail reminder notices at least five days in advance. Make your notices attractive and exciting, and be sure to include the date, time and place.

● Write down each meeting's agenda. Make complete notes on the information and topics you wish to cover. If other individuals will lead parts of the meeting, give them plenty of advance notice.

● Make a list of all the supplies you will need for each meeting. Secure important curriculum items such as teacher materials, the *Champions Music* CD, CD player, etc.

● Plan to serve refreshments. Refreshments show volunteers you appreciate their attendance. The refreshments can be as simple as coffee, tea and cookies or as involved as theme-oriented munchies (popcorn, sports drinks, etc.).

© 2004 Gospel Light. Permission to photocopy granted. *Raising Up Spiritual Champions*

• Purchase or make name tags for all your volunteers to wear at meetings—don't assume volunteers will know each other. Provide a sign-in sheet to give your volunteers a sense of accountability and to make sure you have an accurate record of who has completed training.

• Show appreciation to your volunteers by giving each participant gifts such as candy, sports-themed note pads and/or tote bags.

Tip 3: Follow These Hints for a Successful Meeting

• Arrive early. Having everything planned and set up in advance provides a positive example for your volunteers. You can't expect your volunteers to do more than you're willing to do yourself.

• Play music from the *Champions Music* CD to build excitement. Reinforce the sports theme through the use of decorations, attire, refreshments, prizes, etc.

• Provide some time for fellowship. Start each meeting with an icebreaker game to help your volunteers get to know each other and build friendships and to foster team unity.

• Make the meetings worthwhile. Though "fun" can be on the agenda, be sure to cover important topics in a clear, interesting and timely manner so that volunteers do not feel you have wasted their time!

• Start and end meetings on time. This shows your volunteers that you respect their schedules. Allow about five minutes for volunteers to arrive before beginning the meeting.

© 2004 Gospel Light. Permission to photocopy granted. *Raising Up Spiritual Champions*

Publicity Ideas

Posters

Use one of the logos on page 185 (or print it from the CD-ROM) to make posters telling information about the **Raising Up Spiritual Champions** program. Display the posters in a variety of locations around your church.

Sunday School Visits

Visit upper elementary or middle school classes to describe the **Raising Up Spiritual Champions** program and invite interested children to attend. Send information to children's parents.

Church Website

Add information about **Raising Up Spiritual Champions** to your church's website. Consider adding an online registration feature and a course outline and schedule that will help parents become familiar with the course.

Information Booth

Decorate a booth or table in the church lobby from which to recruit the coaches and trainers and pre-register children. Display a **Raising Up Spiritual Champions** logo and decorate with a sports motif. Prepare promotional flyers, registration forms and volunteer sign-up sheets (see samples in the Forms section of this book) for use at the booth.

Countdown

In your church bulletin, in the lobby of your church or in another public area, create a countdown poster during the eight weeks prior to the beginning of **Raising Up Spiritual Champions:** "Only 24 more days till **Raising Up Spiritual Champions** begins. Join the team!" Provide information about who should join the team, where and when the course will take place and how to register at the bottom of the poster. Update the countdown portion of the poster weekly.

Preseason Play Day

Prepare for and publicize the upcoming **Raising Up Spiritual Champions** course by a promotional event: Champions' Preseason Play Day. Because this course is for a specific group of children within the children's ministry, this event can provide a great opportunity to meet, talk with and register team members and their parents as well as building the enthusiasm of children, their families and the church. (Remember the goal of building community!) Ask your children's ministry director for a roster of those who have made commitments to Christ in the past year or who are in the process of finishing elementary school from which to "prospect." Champions' Preseason Play Day may include fun recreational games, activities such as creating a room mural (see p. 23) and eating sports-related snacks.

© 2004 Gospel Light. Permission to photocopy granted. *Raising Up Spiritual Champions*

Room Decorations

Raising Up Spiritual Champions can take place in any number of venues. But no matter where you choose to hold your program, decorating the rooms where the action will take place can add fun and excitement to the proceedings! Here are some ideas for setting the stage to create the perfect atmosphere for fun and learning.

General sports-related decorations. Before the course, invite your congregation to loan or donate sports-related items. Include any or all of the following: sports posters, team-name hats, foam hands, team visors, pom-poms in team colors, sports jerseys, bobble-head dolls of sports players, small basketball goal and foam basketball, gym bags to hold supplies, etc.

If you cannot leave decorations on the walls from week to week, consider simply pinning sports jerseys and other items to rolling bulletin boards to be brought in during the sessions or sew these items to a sheet that can then be hung on a wall during each session!

Create a place. Name and label one or more rooms, especially if you are using more than one room or are

© 2004 Gospel Light. Permission to photocopy granted. *Raising Up Spiritual Champions*

using a center method with this course. Places such as Training Room or Tournament Stadium can give you and your students some intriguing "handles" for thinking about sports teams and God's team, the Body of Christ. Decorate each room appropriately. Here are two ideas:

Training Room

Create a mural of people in training: lifting weights, riding stationary bikes and working out (people shapes could be created by drawing outlines around posing students). Add appropriate props, such as duffel bags, small weights, stationary bikes, etc.

Tournament Stadium

Create murals of football goalposts or soccer goals at either end of the room. Make a mural that features a view from the sports field of the assembled crowd in the stands. Add murals of concession stands, too! Cheerleaders could be drawn with real pom-poms added for a 3-D effect. Add plastic turf to one or two areas of the room for fun!

Preseason play. To increase awareness and interest, invite prospective team members to a special preseason play event during which they create a large sports-related or place-related mural on bulletin-board paper or large butcher paper. This will build each student's interest and simply but effectively gives the space flair and flavor!

Follow-Up Ideas

What might happen if a generation of adults took personal responsibility for the spiritual development of the next generation? What if there were adults willing to continue to *teach*, encourage, *assist* and *mentor* a group of kids beyond church time? Do you think it would make both a temporal and an eternal difference?

Being a coach for this eight-week discipleship intensive can be one of the most rewarding tasks your volunteers may experience. And the good news is that the relationships your coaches build and the mentoring they begin with the team members can continue! Certainly, it's important to build a team during the course and to give kids a sense of community during these eight weeks. But what if the team leader kept the team together and remained interested in these kids' spiritual lives?

An interested, caring adult whose vision for what a kid can become in Christ could create a revolution in the Church and in the world! A relationship with a caring adult can provide a platform for a young believer to continue to grow and to see following Jesus as a lifelong process. The small, regular investments your coaches make in the lives of individual kids will pay huge eternal dividends!

Daily Devotions

After completing **Raising Up Spiritual Champions**, help your team members continue developing discipleships habits. Send one of the Daily Devotions, found on pages 189-191, to team members each week.

Here is an action plan and some specific ways to encourage coaches to continue the relationships with the kids whom God has put on their teams:

● Motivate coaches by letting them know that when the course is over, their involvement does not have to end. The relationships developed during the course provide a perfect launching pad for further ministry.

● Encourage coaches to learn about their kids. During the eight weeks, ask coaches to make a few notes about each team member—decisions made, interests expressed, service projects done, prayer requests made. This information will help coaches know each child as a person.

● Pray for your coaches and remind them to pray for their kids, asking God to bring to their minds appropriate ways to keep in touch with them and to nurture them in Christ.

● Suggest that coaches use e-mail to stay in touch with team members. (Some kids find talking on the phone a little scary.)

● Schedule several team alumni events over the course of the coming year. It need not be elaborate—a potluck picnic after church, a Saturday breakfast, lunch at a fast-food restaurant, a hike or an afternoon playing board games. Send out postcards or make phone calls. Keep it simple so that coaches can focus on spending time with the kids, letting them know that they are interested in their lives, needs and potential!

● Plan an activity or project (fund-raiser walk, church project, mission trip, etc.) in which kids and coaches can participate as a team!

● Continue the team spirit with a small-group Bible study that meets once or twice a month. Even a meeting once a month will provide all of you with a way to keep up with each others' lives, study God's Word and pray for each other—all those skills you learned together during this course!

© 2004 Gospel Light. Permission to photocopy granted. *Raising Up Spiritual Champions*

Coaching Tips

In this section you will find informative articles dealing with issues of concern to your volunteers. Use these articles in both preventive and prescriptive form: for staff training before problems occur and as a remedy to problem situations already in place.

Just photocopy or print from the CD-ROM the articles of your choice and distribute.

Benefits of Building Relationships

When we adults are focused on the details of getting through a teaching session, it can be easy to forget that no matter how good our activities or how important our points, *nothing* transforms a life more effectively than building a relationship! Relationship is the very reason Christ came to Earth, died and rose again—to make it possible for us to live in *relationship*, first with God the Father through Him and then with each other by the power of His Spirit! Relationship is the hallmark of God's kingdom.

Why Relate?

● **Need.** On any given day, a youngster may enter your session tremendously stressed. Even church kids aren't immune to trauma such as a recent move, the death of a loved one, a lack of food or shelter, separation, divorce, substance abuse or even child abuse. We never know where a child has been emotionally and spiritually. It is imperative that *every* child be given loving acceptance, hugs, smiles and genuine interest! Often the child who displays the most negative behavior is the one who needs the greatest measure of loving acceptance and positive interest.

● **Opportunity.** Because most schoolteachers are overburdened and unable to focus on individual children, school generally cannot make up for a lack of relationship at home. However, we have the opportunity to minister to children through relationship! As we first see each child as a real person made in God's image and then touch, talk and encourage each one as a person worthy of our respect and love, every child understands what God's love looks like, sounds like and feels like.

● **Unity.** Coming from different neighborhoods, children in a church may not know each other well. We can gently help them learn how to build relationships with each other in a safe environment where relationship is valued highly. Children need to know that church is not like any other place they go: This is a place where people love them and love each other. Here, they find people whom they can love freely and safely. There is no better place to begin building a genuine unity in the Body of Christ than here!

Why Care?

● Paul instructed in 1 Corinthians 11:1, "Follow my example, as I follow the example of Christ." Our job is to show, rather than tell, what it means to live as a follower of Jesus. As we are honest, kind and transparent with children, they will get to know us. They will begin to unconsciously identify with and imitate the Christlike character, beliefs and values they see. Our smiles, our touches, our hugs and our gracious reactions to surprising situations often teach more effectively what it means to live as a Christian than even good curriculum or excellent activities.

© 2004 Gospel Light. Permission to photocopy granted. *Raising Up Spiritual Champions*

• As we help children get to know and appreciate each other, we are also leading them to experience the Church, the Body of Christ. Children have the chance to know firsthand that believers in Jesus live and work together as a team, living in sympathy and harmony, instead of the competition, fear and bitterness so commonly found outside God's family.

• We benefit as we know these children! Not only do we become better teachers by understanding their needs and feelings, but we also have the delightful privilege of seeing the world from their perspective!

Through them, God often gives us surprising insights that help us understand Christ's edict that we come to His kingdom as children.

Ways to Show You Care

Make it a rule that these three behaviors welcome every child:

1. A genuine smile that says, "I'm glad to see you today!"

2. Conversation and attention to what the child says at his or her eye level

3. A kind touch on the shoulder or a "safe" one-armed hug

Welcoming children as they enter should be a regular job for one or two people every week. This makes sure that everyone builds a relationship with a safe, caring, friendly adult. Don't leave this important job unassigned! Such relationship building is the foundation of teaching God's Word in real, practical ways!

© 2004 Gospel Light. Permission to photocopy granted. *Raising Up Spiritual Champions*

Bible Memory—Help!

In days gone by, children were expected to memorize a great deal of information. Many lived up to the expectation quite nicely. Having memorized anything from a Scripture to a list of numbers in a foreign language, the successful memorizer was usually given great adult attention and a star on a chart that let everyone know his or her success. Today, kids formally memorize far less (so much information is at our fingertips), and more often they memorize in a context (as in memorizing complicated sequences of video game codes because it's too much trouble to look it up).

Memorizing Scripture, of course, is a very different kind of memorizing from the old-fashioned goal of rote memorization. Our goal is for every child not only to have the words in mind but also to understand the sense of what those words are saying. Like memorizing complicated sequences of game codes, we want to have God's Word right where we can access it when we need it!

While those who memorize easily may well expect stars on their charts, memorizing these verses may present a frightening challenge for some. Use the tips beginning on this page to make memorizing less scary so that each child can see that these verses have value for him or her—not just for those who are used to garnering memory awards.

Here are some tips for helping each child memorize God's Word with understanding:

● As you talk, refer to phrases and ideas from the Bible verse. Tell how knowing these words (or another part of God's Word) has affected your life or helped you make a decision.

● Ask open-ended questions to gain feedback about what kids do or do not understand about the verse. Quite often, a misconception can be cleared up easily if we take time to find out what is not clear.

● Write out a passage or verse on a piece of paper or poster board, breaking it into phrases or concepts as you go. This gives a series of visual cues and provides possible inspiration for putting the words to a tune, to creating a rap or adding motions that will involve kids so that it's easier to remember the words.

● Encourage learners to express their understanding of a Bible verse: draw or paint a picture of what they think the words mean, tell what the verse might

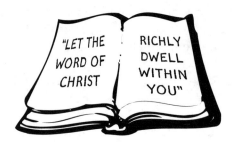

"LET THE WORD OF CHRIST RICHLY DWELL WITHIN YOU"

mean in their own lives, write the verse in their own words or make up a puppet story about a time when it might be important to remember the verse.

● Rather than attempt to motivate learners through a contest or a chart (which will inevitably embarrass some of them), challenge them to work together toward a goal. Offer the group a pizza party when everyone has memorized the verse. (Motivation will skyrocket when you offer a group reward that your kids value!)

Two final points:

1.   Remember that your model will go a long way to encourage your learners' own efforts. If you do not already know the verse (or know it in a different version), memorize along with them! You'll be amazed at the strategies you can come up with when you yourself have to memorize!

2.   Remember that the long-term goal here is to hide God's Word in our hearts. As you place value on that by your own memorizing, your encouragement and your gentle help to make each child successful, the children will understand that remembering God's Word is better than remembering the complicated codes to their favorite games!

© 2004 Gospel Light. Permission to photocopy granted. *Raising Up Spiritual Champions*

Boys and Girls: Are They Compatible?

"Oh no! Here they come!" a sixth-grade girl groans as two boys approach the classroom. But a huge smile lights up her face as she says the words.

"Yuck! You've got cooties!" Generations of preteen boys and girls have accused each other of being infested with these small, invisible insects.

The years before the onset of adolescence seem to be the time when young people are most openly antagonistic toward peers of the opposite sex. Some of the tension between girls and boys is the result of a growing self-awareness and sexual identity. And some is the result of anxiety over a growing awareness of and curiosity about gender differences.

The typical pattern of at least occasional conflict poses significant challenges for the teacher of preteens.

Challenges

Boys and girls may resist sitting next to or working with members of the opposite sex.

● Many girls and boys have significantly different interests and preferred ways of interacting.

● As adolescence approaches, girls tend to mature more rapidly than boys. A group with both fifth and sixth graders is likely to have noticeable differences in maturity levels between older girls and younger boys.

● Verbal put-downs of each other are common ways to cover nervousness and attraction.

● Both boys and girls at this age tend to be intolerant of those who are different from them.

Some teachers, when confronted by these challenges, choose the path of least resistance and completely separate girls and boys. However, same-sex groups have their own set of problems:

© 2004 Gospel Light. Permission to photocopy granted. *Raising Up Spiritual Champions*

• Another set of behavior challenges (i.e., a group of boys getting wild; a group of girls getting silly and giggling), which can be at least as hard to deal with as those faced in a combined-sex group are likely to develop;

• Certain "chemical combinations" (two or more kids who are great as individuals but disruptive when they are together) are more likely to combust without the mediating influence of the other gender;

• Kids do not learn to get along with the other sex;

• Kids are likely to miss out on positive relationships with adults of both sexes. Preteens need the opportunity to be part of a group guided by both women and men.

Consider the following four suggestions to minimize the above challenges while helping girls and boys learn to accept and appreciate each other:

1. Plan ways to mix boys and girls in small-group activities.

If you tell a fifth-grade boy to sit next to a sixth-grade girl, or vice versa, you are likely to hear vociferous protests. Instead, invite both girls and boys to get involved in an interesting activity. When children enjoy being busily occupied, they are unlikely to create a fuss over who happens to be working alongside. Or simply state, "Just for now you need to be in this group. Later you can choose whom you work with."

2. Minimize competition between the sexes.

Preteens love contests and games (as long as they win more often than they lose). Also, a great deal of energy can be generated by challenging the girls to outdo boys and encouraging the boys to best the girls. However, be sparing and cautious with such competitive endeavors, for they contribute to an adversarial attitude rather than fostering acceptance and cooperation.

3. Provide both male and female role models.

Boys and girls need positive relationships with both men and women who respect and support each other. If your teaching staff is all male or all female, regularly involve other adults in your class sessions. Invite parents or others in the congregation to visit your class. Consider these suggestions for ways to involve guests:

• Interview guests about interesting life experiences.
• Ask guests to provide and serve a snack.
• Enlist a guest's help with a learning activity.
• Ask a guest to present a special talent (music, dramatic reading, photography, art, cooking, etc.).

4. Keep your sense of humor.

Rather than being offended when a preteen says something derogatory about "yucky boys" or "gross girls," keep the atmosphere light. Your positive example, and your acceptance of all students, will go a long way toward building healthy attitudes between boys and girls.

© 2004 Gospel Light. Permission to photocopy granted. *Raising Up Spiritual Champions*

Discipline: Our Goal and Our Actions

The Goal

Adults often say in exasperation, "That kid needs some *discipline*!" Now *Merriam-Webster's Collegiate Dictionary* defines "discipline" as "training that corrects, molds, or perfects the mental faculties or moral character."[1] But let's take our definition even further. Let's refer to God's perspective on discipline. Let's look to Jesus!

How did Jesus correct and mold *adults* (who often did not live up to His expectations) and bring them to a place of completeness or maturity? Jesus *discipled* or *disciplined* men whom He trained with a clear goal in mind: to become mature in Him, ready to take His Word all over the world. How did He train these men? By keeping control? By giving out punishment? By making rules? No. He did it by living with them!

Before anything else, Jesus gave His disciples a walking, talking, listening, doing *example* of what He wanted them to become. Jesus knew how we humans always respond to actions more than we do to words alone! The disciples watched, listened and then followed what they had seen and heard from Jesus! Actions always speak more loudly than words alone.

So what should be our goal for discipline? While we might *control* children by other means (fear, guilt or manipulation), such control fails to produce any understanding or self-discipline! "Good discipline" is not about something we do *to* a child but what we do *with* and *for* him or her. The goal of good discipline is to build a relationship with each child so that we can help that child grow in knowing and doing what is good. Relationships are the first step in creating a positive atmosphere for learning in the way Jesus' disciples did!

Effective Methods of Discipline

Acceptance. Children (and adults!) need to feel that someone cares about them and that they are people of worth and value. When we offer loving acceptance (regardless of a person's behavior), we form the foundation for positive discipline. Since our personal goal

© 2004 Gospel Light. Permission to photocopy granted. *Raising Up Spiritual Champions*

should be to grow as disciples of Jesus ourselves, here is a concrete way to love as Jesus does—unconditionally!

When a child enters the room, show him or her the same respect and friendliness you would show to an adult. Address the child by name. Listen attentively to what he or she has to say. A smile, a hand on the shoulder, a pat or a one-armed hug say, "You're important to me. I care about you."

When behavior goes out of bounds, focus on the behavior itself, not on the child. Without scolding or shaming, kindly redirect the behavior. Phrase your directions positively so that the child knows what to do, not just what *not* to do. "Chris, please pass the ball to Mia so that she can take her turn. It's kind to let everyone have a turn. Thanks."

Telling Chris he is a bad boy or giving him a list of reasons why he is doing wrong will not help him refocus and know how to change. Kindness, clear directions and choices within limits will help any child learn good discipline!

Modeling. Children watch constantly. If they hear you talk about how important it is to pick up trash but see you drop paper on the ground, expect them to drop paper, too. Your actions teach far more than the words you say. (Remember Jesus and His disciples!)

Involvement. Children feel comfortable and successful when they know the routine. However, variety within the limits of routine keeps everyone's mind engaged! Provide a variety of ways to catch children's interest and keep them involved: Ask an intriguing question, do something in a new way, prepare a hands-on project or play a game that involves children's minds as well as their bodies. When children are fully involved, discipline problems are less likely to occur.

Adequate space. If you expect children to work and move without bumping into each other, be sure your room provides enough space. Think of ways to rearrange items so that children can move more easily. Decide what can be cleaned up or discarded so that the room has adequate space for each child.

Responding to Unacceptable Behavior

With all of our best examples, our finest relationship building and our most loving intentions, there will still be moments when a child misbehaves in a way that requires immediate intervention. For discipline to be the teaching tool that it should be, consequences need to be clear, immediate and linked to the behavior. Here are some examples:

Misusing materials. Calmly and simply state a reason we don't misuse the materials. "We all will need the scissors later. I can't let you break them. Thanks for putting them back into the basket." If the offender does not correct his or her behavior, give him or her a choice: "You may choose to either leave the scissors in the basket or choose to sit at the far table where there are no scissors." Be sure that either choice is fine with you. If a student insists on continuing, simply say, "I see you chose not to do either. Now it's my turn to choose. It's time for you to (sit at the far table, go with a helper to find your parent, etc.)." Be sure the consequence is carried out and that the offender understands that the consequence was his or her choice.

Offensive words, verbal aggression. "Part of our job here is to help each other be the best followers of Jesus we can be! That's why we use kind words. That did not sound like a kind word to me. What's another way Josh could say that?" When you say kind words to the verbal offender, you teach kindness!

Distracting, clowning. We all like attention. Most of what human beings do is designed to get attention from another person! When a child says something silly, don't make a major issue out of the behavior. Laugh along with them.

When you show that you are not put off by the child's behavior, the behavior loses its power. Then the moment passes and everyone can move on. If a child is distracting others who are trying to listen, first invite a helper to sit close to the child. If distraction persists, give the child a choice of several ways to change the behavior (stop talking, move away from Danny, sit in the chair beside me, etc.). Always make behavior the child's choice.

When we remember the goal of discipline, effective methods of discipline and the power of our own example, discipline becomes the positive tool it is designed to be. It helps both us and our students to grow as disciples of Jesus!

Note
1. *Merriam-Webster's Collegiate Dictionary*, 10th ed., s.v. "discipline."

© 2004 Gospel Light. Permission to photocopy granted. *Raising Up Spiritual Champions*

Get Ready to Coach!

Any person can grab a few materials, run into a classroom to read from a manual, play a game and then send kids on their way. But when we want to coach kids to become wholehearted followers of Jesus Christ, such a teaching method will not work! The method described above displays a dangerous attitude. It says, "You kids don't know the difference. My time and effort are more valuable than you are. I don't need to be prepared for you." And it's not long before the children detect and absorb that unspoken attitude. They conclude that indeed, this is just another program where adults want something from them but where they are not really considered important.

So how can we prepare to be coaches and teachers who are ready to nurture relationships and effectively involve youngsters in life-changing Bible learning? Because we have so little time to teach God's Word to children, we need to be able to "hit the ground running" every time we meet! Mastering the following guidelines will make us prepared to take our teaching times from hesitant to high-energy!

Prepare yourself. One terrific teacher advises, "Begin preparing for the next session as soon as this session is over. Before you close the book, page ahead to see what is coming next. That gives you the rest of the week to think things through, collect materials you otherwise wouldn't have thought of and be relaxed!"

Prepare the Bible content. Don't assume that you know the story! During the week, block out an hour of time to read the Scripture and the Coach's Corner and then pray for the children in your care. Familiarize yourself with the session so that you are able to keep everyone's interest high.

Prepare the environment. Look at your classroom both when full of children and when it is empty. Ask yourself, *What kinds of clutter collect in this room? Where are the bottlenecks where children can't move freely? What items distract children?* Take time to eliminate clutter, rearrange space and make the room an inviting, involving place. If you share a room, meet with those who share the space to work out ways to keep the room functional and inviting.

Prepare the materials. Take a moment to imagine: *What might happen if the kids in my class have to wait because I don't have the materials ready?* It can be very difficult to refocus attention when kids have wandered off both mentally and physically while they wait for an adult to get ready for the next activity. Being prepared is the best defense against wandering attention!

Collect materials and prepare them for the activities ahead of time. Stack materials in the order of use. If your church has a supply room, plan to arrive early enough to gather needed materials before going to your classroom. When you arrive for the session, it's easy to place the stacked, prepared materials in the area of your classroom where they will be used.

© 2004 Gospel Light. Permission to photocopy granted. *Raising Up Spiritual Champions*

Prepare to arrive early. If you've taken the above steps, all that's left to do is some simple setting up when you arrive in the classroom. You've eliminated the panic of doing a lot of preparation in a hurry! Now you are relaxed and ready to focus on the kids instead of on preparation. Because no matter what the stated starting time, any session *really* begins when the first child enters the room! (Yes, this may mean you must be ready to leave home half an hour early. Commit to it as part of your ministry!)

Prepare ways to interact. We quite often can imagine what *we* will be doing during a given part of a session. But a good question to ask is, What will the children be doing during this time? Learn effective and appropriate ways to talk to youngsters. Always have a couple of backup ideas in mind (an intriguing question or a quick game) in case something you have planned doesn't work well. And remember, whenever children are involved in an activity, NEVER sneak away to do something else. These times of activity are another prime opportunity to build relationships and involve children in understanding God's Word!

Time to build relationships with kids and help them become followers of Jesus is at a premium. That's the main reason being prepared is vitally important! When we're prepared to teach and coach, our loving, relaxed attitudes demonstrate God's love to the youngsters we are coaching!

© 2004 Gospel Light. Permission to photocopy granted. *Raising Up Spiritual Champions*

Leading a Good Discussion

Teaching preteens requires a dialogue rather than a monologue. Teachers need to listen as much as—or more than—they speak. However, encouraging students of this age to participate verbally is difficult for some teachers. The following questions about making a discussion truly productive and not a "pooling of ignorance" or an unfocused, rambling conversation are commonly asked.

How do I keep preteens on track in a discussion?

Begin by preparing a few questions that will stimulate students' thinking. Limit the use of questions that require a student to recall information previously received. Knowledge questions (What was Paul's occupation?) do not stimulate interest in the discussion because once the question has been answered, little more can be said. Asking too many knowledge questions can stifle interest and decrease participation of those kids who lack Bible knowledge or confidence in their abilities.

Instead, ask comprehension questions to help students explore the meaning of information. For example, questions such as What do you think was the hardest part about Paul's work? require students to think before they respond. Because comprehension questions do not require right answers, they *encourage* discussion rather than limit it. In fact, each student may suggest a different answer to the question, thus increasing the opportunity for discussion, while keeping the students on track.

Also ask application questions to focus thinking on students' personal situations. For example, "When have *you* felt like Paul must have felt when he was falsely accused?" When Bible truth begins touching a student's daily life, the student will be interested.

How do I get preteens back on track if a digression occurs?

Decide whether the lesson topic is really more important than the digression. If students show a significant interest in whatever drew the group off track, if you feel that topic has real value to the group, and if you feel capable of guiding the group in learning about the new topic, then you may decide to leave your lesson plan and stay with the new issue.

However, if the digression does not warrant a complete change of direction, use questions to bring attention back to the topic and its particular implications. You may restate the original question to

© 2004 Gospel Light. Permission to photocopy granted. *Raising Up Spiritual Champions*

remind students of the issue at hand. Or try rephrasing the question if students' comments indicate they did not understand what you asked them. Or move on to a new question if you feel the students have probably said all they are likely to contribute to the previous question.

It is usually helpful to acknowledge that the group has been off on a tangent. Avoid making a big deal out of it, but be clear that it is time to return to the session topic. A sense of humor at such times will certainly help you avoid a power struggle with students.

How do I handle interruptions?

If no one else seems distracted by the interruption, just keep on going. Remember, preteens tend to be used to situations where several things are going on at once, and a minimal interruption may almost pass unnoticed by everyone else but you.

If the interruption definitely caught the class's attention, acknowledge it as matter-of-factly as possible, and then restate the question being discussed. You may also want to summarize some of the key points already made in the discussion.

How do I know if kids are bored with a discussion, and what should I do about it if they are?

You will never need to wonder if preteens are bored. They will make it very clear, either by announcing loudly, "This is boring!" or by "cutting up" and causing trouble in some fashion. What to do about a boring discussion is another matter.

It is usually best to assume that once boredom has taken hold in a discussion, it is a terminal condition. It is easier to recapture interest with a different activity (e.g., the next thing you had planned to do) than to rejuvenate interest in the same discussion.

What do I do when no one says anything?

If you've asked a thought-provoking question,

assume that students need at least a few moments to think. Rather than getting nervous when your question is greeted by silence, simply say, "I don't want to hear the first idea that pops into your head. Take a few moments and think about it." Then be silent for a bit (no more than 30 seconds), and repeat or rephrase the question. If you still get no response, award yourself 50 points for "Stumping the Experts!" or "Asking a Question No One Has an Answer For!" or some such category. Then give your own answer to the question and move on.

If your students' reluctance to discuss is a recurring problem, take a good look at the questions you have been asking. Are they too vague? Are they threatening? Do they require knowledge the students do not have? Are the answers too obvious?

If the questions are fine, evaluate your response to what the students do say. Are you unwilling to accept students and their answers if they differ from the "correct" responses? Do you have a tendency to always "improve" the students' answers? Work at creating a climate of openness.

Finally, add some variety to your approach in asking questions:

● Have students write their answers on paper. This allows them time to organize their thoughts. Then invite them to read what they wrote.

● Divide the class into smaller groups. You may ask all groups the same questions or assign different questions to each group. Then invite volunteers to share the answers for their groups.

What do I do when kids are only giving pat answers?

Try the same ideas suggested when students do not answer at all. The root problem is often the same in either case: The students do not feel secure sharing what they really think.

© 2004 Gospel Light. Permission to photocopy granted. *Raising Up Spiritual Champions*

Leading a Student to Christ

Many adult Christians look back to their upper-elementary years as the time when they accepted Christ as Savior. Not only are preteens able to understand the difference between right and wrong and their own personal need of forgiveness, they are also interested in Jesus' death and resurrection as the means by which God provides salvation. In addition, children at this age are capable of growing in their faith through prayer, Bible reading, worship and service.

However, preteens are still limited in their understanding and immature in following through on their intentions and commitments. As such, they need thoughtful, patient guidance in coming to know Christ personally and continuing to grow in Him. While we may assume that students in this discipleship course have made the choice to become members of God's family, an opportunity is provided in Sessions 1-6 to talk further with students about salvation.

1. Pray.

Ask God to prepare the students in your group to receive the good news about Jesus and to prepare you to effectively communicate with them.

2. Present the good news.

Use words and phrases that students understand. Avoid any symbolism that will confuse these literal-minded thinkers. *Discuss these points slowly enough to allow time for thinking and comprehending.*

a. God wants you to become His child. Do you know why God wants you in His family? (See 1 John 4:8.)

b. You and all the people in the world have done wrong things and disobeyed God. The Bible word for doing wrong is "sin." What do you think should happen to us when we sin? (See Romans 6:23.)

c. God loves you so much, He sent His Son to die on the cross for your sin. Because Jesus never sinned, He is the only one who can take the punishment for your sin. (See 1 Corinthians 15:3; 1 John 4:14.)

d. Are you sorry for your sin? Tell God that you are. Do you believe Jesus died to take the punishment for your sin and is alive today? If you tell God you are sorry for your sin and tell Him you do believe and accept Jesus' death to take away your sin—God forgives all your sin. (See John 1:12.)

e. The Bible says that when you believe that Jesus is God's Son and that He is alive today, you receive God's gift of eternal life. This gift makes you a child of God. This means God is with you now and forever. (See John 3:16.)

As you give students many opportunities to think about what it means to be a Christian, expose them to a variety of lessons and descriptions of the meaning of salvation to aid their understanding.

3. Talk individually with students.

Talking about salvation one-on-one creates opportunities to ask and answer questions. Ask questions that move the student beyond simple yes-or-no answers or recitation of memorized information. Ask open-ended, "what do you think?" questions such as:

- Why do you think it's important to . . . ?

- What are some things you really like about Jesus?

- Why do you think that Jesus had to die in order for people to be forgiven?

- What difference do you think it makes for a person to be forgiven?

Answers to these open-ended questions will help you discern how much the student does or does not understand.

4. Offer opportunities without pressure.

Preteens are mature in many ways, but still vulnerable to being manipulated by adults. A good way to guard against coercing a student's response is to simply pause periodically and ask, "Would you like to hear more about this now or at another time?" Loving acceptance of the student, even when he or she is not fully interested in pursuing the matter, is crucial in building and maintaining positive attitudes toward becoming part of God's family.

5. Give time to think and pray.

There is great value in encouraging a student to think and pray about what you have said before making a response. Also allow moments for quiet thinking about questions you ask.

6. Respect the student's response.

Whether or not a student declares faith in Jesus Christ, there is a need for adults to accept the student's action. There is also a need to realize that a student's initial responses to Jesus are just the beginning of a lifelong process of growing in the faith.

7. Guide the student in further growth.

Here are three important parts in the nurturing process:

a. *Talk regularly about your relationship with God.* As you talk about your relationship, the student will begin to feel that it's OK to talk about such things. Then you can comfortably ask the student to share his or her thoughts and feelings, and encourage the student to ask questions of you.

b. *Prepare the student to deal with doubts.* Emphasize that certainty about salvation is not dependent on our feelings or doing enough good deeds. Show the student places in God's Word that clearly declare that salvation comes by grace through faith (i.e., John 1:12; Ephesians 2:8,9; Hebrews 11:6; 1 John 5:11).

c. *Teach the student to confess all sin.* To confess means to admit or to agree. Confessing sins means agreeing with God that we really have sinned. Assure the student that confession always results in forgiveness.

© 2004 Gospel Light. Permission to photocopy granted. *Raising Up Spiritual Champions*

Make Your Words Count!

Imagine that you are standing among giants who constantly mumble to each other over your head. Frustrating? Frightening? Indeed! That's similar to what it's like to be a kid in a crowd of talking adults! Although we often talk *at* children, we find that unless we know how to talk effectively *with* them, they seem to tune out our words!

To talk and relate in ways that children understand, follow Jesus' example! What did Jesus do when He was around children? He loved them; He didn't lecture them. He touched them and blessed them. He held them up as examples of what is good. Remember that children need far more action than talk: Actions say far more than words alone ever do. Even kids who don't understand the meanings of all our words are keen observers of body language, facial expression and tone of voice. They will quickly grasp the emotional content of our words.

How to Talk Effectively

● Place yourself where you can look a child in the eye. (Kneel or sit if needed!)

● Look into the child's eyes. (This not only gets the child's attention but also sends the message, "I see you. You're important to me. I care about you.")

● Show a child the same respect you would show an adult as you converse. (Resist the urge to interrupt, finish a thought, put down or talk down! And NO sarcasm!)

● Genuinely smile as you talk. (Avoid that pasted-on smile grown-ups sometimes wear when dealing with children! Children need to see genuine love.)

● Listen without passing judgment. (Children are more likely to think as they are talking. If a child's words seem off base, ask questions as you would with an adult you respect.)

● Use the child's name often. (A child may well assume you are *not* talking to him or her unless you use the child's name!)

● Give a kind touch on the shoulder to express your love as you talk.

● Use these words frequently: "please," "I'm sorry," "that's all right," "I understand," "thank you."

● Use these phrases often: "I'm glad to see you…," "I like the way you…," "I need you to…," "It's time to…"

● Be quick to see and point out what is good. (When you say, "I'm glad to see you helping Josiah,

Kade. That's a way to obey God's Word. Thank you," you've acknowledged one child's positive action, let the child know you appreciate those actions and helped both children see that God's Word relates to what they're doing!)

● When a child refuses to cooperate, give a choice. (Refocus the child and put responsibility for behavior back on him or her. "Nadia, it's time to finish cleanup. Would you like to put those markers away yourself or would you like to choose a friend to help you?" Offer choices that are perfectly acceptable either way.)

What to Avoid

● Don't use sarcasm! (Sarcasm is always based on the idea that "I'm smarter than you." Kids will likely feel belittled by the tone of voice alone.)

● Don't overexplain. (Keep explanations short and to the point.)

● Don't exaggerate. (Part of your job is to help kids understand how the world works. Don't confuse or abuse kids' trust by telling them anything untrue— not even if you plan to tell them later it was a joke. Take the power of your own words seriously!)

● Don't label. (Statements such as, "You're a lot of trouble!" shut down communication. Focus on the behavior, not the child. Help the child correct problem behavior by giving choices and positive directions. Labeling calls a child's value into question.)

● Don't correct what you *think* a child is saying or finish his or her sentence or thought.

● Don't indulge in negative nonverbal signals. (Sighing, looking away, glancing at your watch tell the child clearly that you are not listening. Would you behave that way if Jesus were talking with you?)

Remember that whenever you talk with a child, you can in some way communicate God's love to him or her. Use the opportunity!

© 2004 Gospel Light. Permission to photocopy granted. *Raising Up Spiritual Champions*

Spiritual Development of Third Through Sixth Graders

When leading a course on discipleship, it's important that we understand the spiritual development of the children we teach! Just as every child grows at his or her own unique pace along the spectrum of physical and mental development, so also are there wide variations in children's spiritual development. Every learner's situation is uniquely influenced by his or her home environment, the stability of his or her family and his or her previous exposure to Bible learning.

Because children learn about life through firsthand experience, it is through living (not listening!) that they come to understand what life is about. From those experiences they then build a frame of reference by which they understand new ideas. Because a child's frame of reference is limited to what he or she has experienced in life, it's important for us to connect God's Word to those life experiences so that a child will have a better chance to make sense of the largely abstract ideas that are part of Bible learning.

Here are some general characteristics of the thinking and spiritual readiness of youngsters 8 to 12 years of age.

Third and Fourth Graders

Expect that some third and fourth graders will be quite able to tell you details of a Bible story or quote a Bible memory verse. They may have developed skills in finding Bible verses and quoting the names of the books of the Bible. However, because their conceptual thinking skills are still developing, they may have difficulty connecting those stories or words to their own life situations without guidance.

Since that limited frame of reference colors their understanding of right and wrong, they may not see some behaviors as sinful. For instance, a younger third-grade boy may say that if his sister did wrong, he would not tell his parents—not from a desire to disobey the parents, but because he's been taught that protecting his sister is the right thing to do. To reconcile both ideas is yet beyond him.

As they mature, third and fourth graders begin to realize that there may be valid opinions besides their own and are less likely to hang on to one point of view (as above). It's helpful to remember that what we may see as stubbornness may simply indicate that child's level of development!

Third and fourth graders are open to sensing their need for God's help and may have an awareness of sin. They can recognize their need for a relationship with Jesus Christ and may be interested in joining God's family.

• Encourage third and fourth graders to discover information in the Bible on their own and help them learn and use their Bible skills successfully. Ask open-ended questions to help them formulate answers related to their own lives based on what they read in the Bible.

• Let children know that your classroom is a safe place. Make it clear that kindness is the rule. Unkind words or actions are not part of the gatherings in this course. Rather, focus children on working together to help each other become wholehearted followers of Jesus.

• Use the small-group times to help children build relationships and feel more comfortable with each other and with you. Model the love and acceptance God has shown you: Children need to *see* how God affects our actions so that they can understand what a living relationship with God looks, sounds and behaves like!

© 2004 Gospel Light. Permission to photocopy granted. *Raising Up Spiritual Champions*

Fifth and Sixth Graders

Fifth and sixth graders can vary tremendously. Not only is the spectrum of physical and emotional development wide, but also the variety in background and experience may make some youngsters seem very sophisticated while others seem quite young. (Sixth graders who are in middle school may especially exhibit that "11 going on 22" look. But they are not as sophisticated as they look!)

Fifth and sixth graders are increasingly verbal. They are gaining greater ability to do abstract thinking and are more and more able to reason out ethical decisions and apply God's Word to some of their circumstances. They can express their feelings and ideas well. However, they aren't as likely to "think aloud" as a younger child might. So it's important to listen with kindness and interest (foregoing judgment on their words) to keep the lines of communication open. The threat of embarrassment can create a silence that quickly eliminates any real discussion in a group. Guide discussions in such a way that you make it clear that you respect their efforts to become thinking people.

Fifth and sixth graders often have a good grasp of what's in the Bible and can have deep feelings of love for God. They may be ready to share the good news of Jesus with another person. Because they have moved into abstract thinking, they have a better grasp of the big picture of what goes on at church and how it relates to God's kingdom. They are beginning to increasingly think of others.

● Avoid lecturing. Give fifth and sixth graders plenty of chances to respond and interact in a variety of ways (art, discussion, games, etc.). We adults are tempted to talk more because kids this age can sit quietly and may appear to listen. But they often tune out adult lectures while appearing interested!

● Treat them with all the respect you would show an adult and all the tenderness you would show a toddler. They want to feel grown-up, yet they are fragile emotionally.

● Plan and utilize chances for youngsters this age to make choices and decisions based on their understanding of the Bible concepts. Help them plan specific ways to apply in everyday life the biblical truths they are learning.

● Plan service projects that give them a chance to live out the principles they are learning in the Bible.

© 2004 Gospel Light. Permission to photocopy granted. *Raising Up Spiritual Champions*

Sports Talk

This course uses sports terminology to help clarify the process of discipleship. Sports and sports training give us some familiar mental "hooks" on which to hang our understanding because we already understand how we learn to play a sport! First, we watch and imitate (follow) a player (a discipler) who is more skilled (mature) than we currently are. After all, we become like what we look at! So our focusing and application (looking and imitating) help us improve our skills and even our attitudes, since attitude is more often "caught" than taught.

Second, we understand how strength training gives us endurance, the ability to "go the distance" when a competition or contest (spiritual test) comes. We recognize how our consistent practice of any skill can make us even better at what we do, even if we are complete novices now.

Paul tells Timothy to "train yourself to be godly. For physical training is of some value, but godliness has value for all things" (1 Timothy 4:7-8). Our goal here is to become humble models worth following, able to coach our team members in ways to be effective as they train and practice in a program where each and every one can be wildly successful—no athletic skill is required! This may well be a place where success can build on success for some disciples who are not involved in a sport or who don't feel confident in other areas.

By hanging the steps of discipleship on sports terms, we hope to convey clearly the ways we watch, learn, imitate and practice to move us all along in the process of becoming all-star disciples of Jesus. Each one is an MVP to Him!

Teaching Kids to Pray

One of the most challenging tasks facing a teacher of preteens is how to build a climate where students will be comfortable praying in the group. In order for preteens to make prayer a meaningful part of their daily lives, they need group prayer experiences to provide positive patterns they can imitate.

1. Keep your own prayers simple, brief and personal.

Your students need to see you pray. Just as Jesus' example motivated His disciples to want to learn to pray (see Luke 11:1), you are a model of prayer for the students you teach. They need to hear prayers that they can duplicate. They also need to hear prayers that really matter to you, not mere formalities or vague declarations. Thus, you must become transparent to your class, sharing some of your doubts, struggles and anxieties.

2. Focus prayer time on issues of concern to the class.

If you want students to care about prayer, then pray for what they already care about. Listen to their conversations to gain insight into issues and events that concern and interest them. Ask them to tell what they enjoy or what causes them worry. Demonstrate an attitude of interest and caring as you talk with preteens about the items they share. Then pray with them about those concerns. (NOTE: Some of the most meaningful prayer times occur one-on-one when a student mentions something in informal conversation and a teacher offers right then to pray about it.)

3. Structure prayer as conversation with God.

Avoid making prayer a recitation of problems for God to solve. Establish a model of talking with God about the good and the bad, the fun and the serious, the joys and the sorrows of life. Avoid archaic language and

© 2004 Gospel Light. Permission to photocopy granted. *Raising Up Spiritual Champions*

Christian jargon. Preteens need to experience communication with God that is both respectful and highly personal.

4. Invite students to suggest items to pray about.

Once you have established a pattern of openly talking about and informally praying for things of importance to your students, then encouraging students to suggest prayer requests becomes very meaningful. Without the foundation of supportive, personal sharing, asking students to mention things to pray about has a tendency to elicit a litany of "safe" requests (Grandma's bad knee, dead goldfish, etc.) or announcements about upcoming events ("Pray for my birthday party on Tuesday afternoon."). Elicit prayer requests about the lesson topic by asking questions such as When is a time you need God's help in saying only good things about others?

5. Invite volunteers to each pray for one item.

Students who are comfortable with mentioning things to pray about are not threatened by praying aloud for one of those items—especially if a pattern of simple, brief prayers has already been set.

Guidelines for Building Kids' Prayer Lives

1. Make prayer an important time in your class session. If classroom prayer is haphazard, boring or an add-on after everything else is done, students will not be drawn to want to pray on their own.

2. Share incidents from your own prayer experiences. Talk with your class about your own prayer times during the week. When do you pray? What did you pray about this week? What benefits do you feel you gained from your prayer times?

3. Ask "What can I pray about for you this next week?" When you talk informally with preteens, before, during or after class, make a point of finding out what is happening in their lives. Then let them know you'll make a point of praying about that in the next few days.

4. Ask "What have you been praying about this past week?" Once your students are familiar with prayer in your classroom and your example of personal prayer, encourage them to pray on their own. One way to do this is to suggest that each student choose to pray during the week for one concern raised by

"LET THE WORD OF CHRIST RICHLY DWELL WITHIN YOU"

class members. Then make a point to ask students about their previous weeks' prayer experiences.

5. Encourage prayer journals. Preteens can gain a great deal of satisfaction from a written record of their prayer times. Provide small notebooks for each student to use in writing a few sentences after each prayer. The journal may contain prayer requests and answers, but it should focus on the student's thoughts and feelings about prayer.

Ideas for Ways to Vary Prayer Time

1. Silent prayer. Suggest one thing for everyone to pray about silently; then allow 15-20 seconds of silence. Encourage students to talk about this prayer experience. Many people find it difficult to focus their attention when all is quiet. One approach students may try is to imagine themselves bowing before God as He asks, "What do you want to say to Me right now?"

2. Completion prayers. One at a time, suggest a variety of prayer sentences students can complete: "I praise You, God, because . . . ," "You have been good to me by . . . ," "One problem I need Your help with is . . . ," "Please help me not to be worried about . . . ," etc. Complete each sentence yourself; then invite volunteers to offer their own completions.

3. Conversational prayer. Invite students to talk to God as they would to a close friend. Suggest these three rules:

• Pray about just one thing, and then give someone else a turn.

• Before you pray about something else, tell God what you think about what the previous person just said.

• Talk to God about what's going on in your life. Don't just keep asking for things.

4. Build a prayer. Either on handout sheets or lettered on the chalkboard or a poster, provide a variety of different prayer statements from which students can choose. Include two or more options for each part of a prayer: the address, praise for who God is, thanks for what He has done, prayer for others, personal requests and closing. For example, options for the address could be "Dear God," "Dear Father in heaven," "Awesome God," etc.

5. Written prayers. Putting thoughts and feelings in writing is often less threatening than speaking them aloud. After prayers have been written, invite volunteers to read at least part of what they wrote. Respect the right of confidentiality in these prayers.

6. Pray as you go. Rather than compiling a list of requests and praises and then praying about them,

invite a volunteer to pray for each item as it is mentioned.

7. Topical prayers. Focus prayers on a particular theme or topic, preferably related to the day's lesson or to a current issue of major interest to students. For example, when studying about serving others, lead the class in prayers of thanks for those who have served them, in prayers for development of willing attitudes to serve and in prayers for awareness of opportunities to be of service.

© 2004 Gospel Light. Permission to photocopy granted. *Raising Up Spiritual Champions*

Understanding Learning Styles

God made each of us unique and He loves our uniqueness! Even in the way we learn new information, each of us is different. Every person develops a cluster of ways to learn that works best for him or her. When we understand these learning styles, we are better able to plan and provide experiences to best help children learn, feel successful and know that God loves each of them as unique people!

While the list below constantly expands as research continues, these broad descriptions will help get you started. First read the following descriptions to recognize your own learning styles: These affect the way you choose the activities you plan. Then read the descriptions again while considering the learning styles and strengths of both the teachers and the learners in your group.

Visual

Visual learners learn best when there is something to look at! They usually are eager to read, draw and write because they want to *see* the information. They may enjoy worksheets and prefer complete quiet to background music or sound. They are bothered by visual clutter and prefer an orderly looking environment. (It's estimated that most schoolteachers are primarily visual learners!)

Verbal

Verbal learners learn best by talking and conversing. They process ideas best by talking about them; they like to listen (especially if they can talk, too!). They better remember things that are set to music. They like to have music or sound in the background; visual clutter doesn't bother them. They ask many questions, not because they weren't paying attention, but because they want more understanding. While verbal learners may seem too talkative or distracting, their learning style challenges us to provide opportunities to talk and listen so that they learn effectively!

Kinesthetic and Tactile

Kinesthetic learners learn best when their bodies are in motion. They process information with their whole bodies! They may often use their hands as they talk or may act out what they say.

Tactile learners learn well through touching and handling. They like to take things apart. They fiddle with things constantly and learn far more by *doing* than by seeing or hearing.

Kinesthetic and tactile learners respond well to touches and hugs. They learn best in a cozy environment with soft lighting. Hands-on activities that involve more than one sense help them learn best, as do large-muscle activities, such as games or actions to help them remember a word.

© 2004 Gospel Light. Permission to photocopy granted. *Raising Up Spiritual Champions*

Relational and Reflective

Relational learners are keen observers. They notice the body language and tone of voice of those around them. They first pick up the emotional content and then process information by realizing how people feel and by responding to those feelings. They like cooperative, interactive activities; they are "people persons," energized by interaction.

Reflective learners, on the other hand, don't shun group activities but they tend to think more about who they are and where they fit. They are acutely aware of their own feelings and are sometimes drained by too much group interaction. They may prefer to express themselves more often through one-person activities.

Logical

To some degree everyone is a logical problem-solver, but some people enjoy problem solving more than others. These learners see the patterns in the world and want to think through a problem to its logical end. They are glad to have point-by-point explanations of how things work, and they enjoy mental challenges. They often count things without being asked to count. They enjoy categorizing and calculating.

Musical

Most people enjoy music in some way, but musical learners are those who tend to be more sensitive to rhythm and pitch and to the musical qualities of spoken language (such as poetry). They tend to be good listeners but probably won't sit still when music plays! They tap rhythms, make up songs on the spot or dance and move to music. They also seem to remember information better when set to music.

This brief overview describes some of the ways we all process new information. When you provide activities that challenge and stimulate children in the ways they learn best, they are more easily engaged, focused and cooperative.

It may not be easy or interesting for you to do some activities because of your own learning styles. But as you understand your own learning styles as well as those of your students, you'll find it worthwhile to try the activities you never thought you'd do!

© 2004 Gospel Light. Permission to photocopy granted. *Raising Up Spiritual Champions*

Sessions

In this section are each session's instructions, Resource Pages (scripts, game cards, etc.), *Student Pages* and *Parent Pages*. Before each session, prepare the Resource Pages as directed in the session. Make a copy of the *Student Page* and *Parent Page* for each team member.

The Coach's Corner

What's a disciple? A long-robed figure listening raptly to Jesus? A person who imitates a role model's every move and word? To a preteen's mind, the word may bring up no image at all. According to the Barna Research Group, 44 percent of preteens say they have no role models.[1] Two out of three also say that spiritual truth can only be discovered through logic, human reason and personal experience—not Scripture.[2] Even preteens who have begun a relationship with Jesus Christ may not yet see ways in which they can follow Jesus as His well-known disciples Peter and John once did.

In this course, our goal is to lead these preteens to become disciples who seek to think and act like Jesus. Colossians 2:6-7 tells us that discipleship is an active process. Disciples don't just sit there, they *do* something! We *receive* Christ as our Savior and Lord. As we *continue to live* in Him, His life sends the roots of our understanding deeper into His Word. He *builds us up* and makes us *strong* spiritually as we continue the process of learning and applying what we are *taught*. His Holy Spirit works in us to fill us with His power so that our lives *overflow* with thankfulness!

Every disciple of Jesus Christ is at some point in this lifelong process. None of us has yet arrived at full maturity! As we begin, we need to evaluate our own need for spiritual exercise and training: What parts of our lives do we still need to yield to God so that we overflow with thankfulness? Which skills do we still need to practice consistently? In these next weeks, we have the exciting opportunity to fulfill the Great Commission here and now—by mentoring and coaching younger members of God's family into wholehearted, all-star disciples of Jesus Christ!

Note: We've designed this course using sports as a theme and using sports terminology. Sports and sports training provide familiar mental hooks on which to hang understanding to help improve both skills and attitudes.

Notes
1. George Barna, *Transforming Children into Spiritual Champions* (Ventura, CA: Regal Books, 2003), p. 24.
2. Ibid, p. 36

Bible Memory Verse

"Just as you received Christ Jesus as Lord, continue to live in him, rooted and built up in him, strengthened in the faith as you were taught, and overflowing with thankfulness."
Colossians 2:6-7

Scripture Study

Mark 1:14-20;
John 1:35-49

Aims:

1. To determine that Jesus' first disciples followed Him to learn about Him

2. To express understanding that being Jesus' disciple means to think and act like Him

3. To plan and practice ways to act as Jesus' disciple

© 2004 Gospel Light. Permission to photocopy granted. *Raising Up Spiritual Champions*

Session Game Plan

WARM-UP (10-20 minutes)

Materials: Large sheet of butcher paper, masking tape, marker.

Procedure: Play a game to show what it means to follow a leader, and then tell ideas for a written list about what it means to be a disciple.

POWER-UP (20-30 minutes)

Materials: Bible for each team member, three copies of "Let Me Tell You!" (pp. 61-64), length of butcher paper, markers, scissors, masking tape.

Procedure: Listen to two followers of Jesus and study the names they gave to Jesus to discover why Jesus' first disciples followed Him.

PRACTICE (20-30 minutes)

Materials: *Session 1 Student Page* (pp. 67-68) for each team member; Strategy Stations (pp. 65-66); trash can or sturdy basket, masking tape, marker, eight index cards and foam ball for every eight team members; scissors; eight large sheets of colored construction paper; markers; pencils.

Procedure: Play a game, review and apply information in preparation to complete a part of the *Student Page*.

RALLY (10-20 minutes)

Materials: *Champions Music* CD and player, each team member's *Session 1 Student Page, Session 1 Parent Page* (pp. 69-70) for each team member, pencils.

Procedure: Sing worship songs, talk about the week's assignment and pray together.

KEEP YOUR BRAINSTORMING POSTERS!

The butcher paper lists and charts made during each class session are valuable records of your team members' thought processes and will be used again during Sessions 7 and 8. Keep posters on the walls, adding new ones each week. If this is not possible, consider using poster board or other sturdy material for longer-lasting posters that will be easy to display and remove.

© 2004 Gospel Light. Permission to photocopy granted. *Raising Up Spiritual Champions*

WARM-UP (10-20 minutes)

Guess the Leader

Materials: Large sheet of butcher paper, masking tape, marker.

Preparation: Tape butcher paper to wall. Write the word "DISCIPLE" in large letters on the paper.

Procedure: Today we're challenging two volunteers to see if they can figure out who in this circle is the leader. Team members stand in a circle. Two volunteers leave the room.

Invite team members to suggest and pantomime a variety of sport actions (pass or catch a football, dribble or shoot a basketball, kick or throw a soccer ball, swing a baseball bat, pitch a baseball, etc.). Then ask for a volunteer to be the leader. The leader then pantomimes a sport action. Others in the circle practice imitating the action without looking directly at the leader so that it is difficult to tell who the leader is. Invite volunteers back to watch the actions. The leader then adds to or changes motions that the group continues to imitate.

Volunteers try to guess both the actions and the leader. (Challenge: Limit observation time to 20 seconds.) Play several rounds, using different volunteers and leaders. Between rounds, ask:

🖋 **How could you tell who the leader was?**

🖋 **What did people in the circle do that showed who the leader was?**

🖋 **When did a leader do something that helped you guess?**

🖋 **Who are some leaders you've seen people follow?**

🖋 **What words might describe a leader you would want to follow?**

A person who follows or imitates a leader in order to learn to be like that leader can be called a disciple. Point to the word "disciple" lettered on butcher paper. **What words or phrases come to your mind when you see the word "disciple"?** Team members tell words or phrases. Write these responses on the butcher paper.

🖋 **What do you think a disciple is?**

🖋 **Why would someone want to be a disciple of another person?**

🖋 **What might someone do to learn how to be a disciple?**

🖋 **What else could you say about being a disciple?**

🖋 **What else would you like to know about being a disciple?**

Conclusion: Today we're going to talk about what it means to follow Jesus and be His disciples.

© 2004 Gospel Light. Permission to photocopy granted. *Raising Up Spiritual Champions*

POWER-UP (20-30 minutes)

Materials: Bible for each team member, three copies of "Let Me Tell You!" (pp. 61-64), length of butcher paper, markers, scissors, masking tape.

Increase interest and interaction! Invite two men to dress as Andrew and Peter and read the script.

Preparation: Print "A disciple follows Jesus every day" in large letters across butcher paper and then cut paper into nine puzzle-like pieces. On the blank side of each puzzle piece, write one of the following references: John 1:35, John 1:38, John 1:51. Write John 1:41, John 1:45, and John 1:49 on two puzzle pieces each.

Procedure: Be sure each team member has a Bible. **Let's find John chapter 1, verse 29.** Give help as needed, encouraging team members to use contents page in Bibles for reference. **During our game, we watched closely to follow the leader. In today's Bible study, we'll hear from two men who watched Jesus closely. These men were the first two disciples to follow Jesus. Let's discover some reasons why they followed Him.**

Designate two team members who read aloud easily to read the script as Andrew and Peter.

After the script has been read, ask these questions:

☺ **Who were some of Jesus' followers mentioned in this script?** (Andrew, John, Peter, James, Philip, Nathanael.)

☺ **What did Andrew and Peter learn about Jesus? How did they learn this information?**

☺ **Who was surprised by Jesus' words? Why?** (Nathanael was surprised because Jesus knew all about him before he met Him.)

☺ **What were some reasons these men wanted to follow Jesus?** (They believed and trusted John the Baptist. They were convinced by what Jesus said and did.)

☺ **How do you think Jesus' words and actions were different from the actions of other people?** (He did things they did not expect. He was kind. His actions convinced them that He was the Messiah.)

The "Let Me Tell You!" script can be reproduced from the CD-ROM or from pages 61-64. You'll need three copies.

© 2004 Gospel Light. Permission to photocopy granted. *Raising Up Spiritual Champions*

Hearing about a person from someone you trust, seeing a person's actions and hearing a person's words are all important ways to know more about a person. But we can find out more about who Jesus is in another way. Turn to John 1:35-49. In these verses, people called Jesus by nine different names. These names can help us understand more about who Jesus is.

Team members form pairs or trios. **Find someone who likes the same kind of (ice cream) as you do.** Distribute one or two puzzle pieces and a marker to each pair. Pairs find and discuss assigned verse and then write next to the verse reference both the name of Jesus they found and what they think the name means. If time is limited, complete activity as a group. When groups have finished, invite them to share the name they found and what they think it means. Supplement explanations as needed (see below). **We discovered some good clues about who Jesus is from these names.** Invite students to fit and then tape puzzle pieces together. Turn over the paper so team members can read sentence.

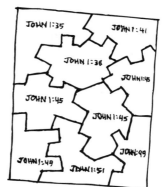
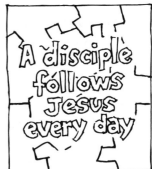

John 1:35—Lamb of God. Jesus was sacrificed to deliver us from sin, just as the first Passover lamb was sacrificed in Egypt to deliver the firstborn sons of the Israelites from death.

John 1:38—Rabbi. The Aramaic or Hebrew word for "teacher." Jesus taught His followers what it means to love God and follow Him.

John 1:41—Messiah. The Hebrew word for "Anointed One," which means the Savior whom God promised to send.

John 1:41—Christ. The Greek word for "Anointed One." Jesus was chosen or anointed by God to be the Savior.

John 1:45—Jesus of Nazareth. Nazareth was the city in which Jesus grew up. "Nazarene" was a synonym for "despised" in Jesus' day.

John 1:45—Son of Joseph. Joseph was the name of Mary's husband.

John 1:49—Son of God. This name tells us that Jesus is God's Son sent from heaven to Earth to demonstrate God's love for us.

John 1:49—King of Israel. This name meant that Jesus is the King who will one day rule over the Jewish people and everyone.

John 1:51—Son of Man. Jesus called Himself the Son of Man many times. It meant that even though He is God's Son, He is also a man who came to Earth to demonstrate God's love for us.

You might also ask, **What other names for Jesus have you heard?** Discuss those names and their meanings.

Conclusion: We've discovered some reasons to follow Jesus from the names He is given in these verses. What are some other reasons you think people follow Jesus today? In your discussion about following Jesus, ask team members to think about whether they have ever made the decision to be a disciple of Jesus and become a member of His family. Invite team members to tell you if they want to talk further about what it means to become a member of God's family. Arrange a time after the session to talk with the team member (see "Leading a Student to Christ" on p. 39).

PRACTICE (20-30 minutes)

1. Look and Follow Drill

Materials: Trash can or sturdy basket, masking tape, marker, eight index cards and foam ball for every eight team members.

Preparation: Set trash can or basket on a table. Make a masking-tape line about 3 feet (.9-m) from the trash can or basket. Write one letter of the word "disciple" on each of the eight index cards and place cards in the trash can or basket. (Prepare one setup for every group of eight team members.)

Procedure: Team members line up behind line and brainstorm ways to toss the ball into trash can (with two hands, over the shoulder, on knees, while turning, etc.).

First team member in line tosses the ball into the trash can as desired, then retrieves it and removes a card from trash can before passing ball to next team member. (If team member misses a shot, he or she takes another turn.)

Next team member imitates previous team member's tossing action (like "faking" in basketball), then tosses the ball into trash can in another way and takes ball and a card from trash can. Team member passes ball to next team member, who imitates that team member's tossing action before tossing ball into trash can in yet another

way. Play continues until everyone has had a turn to toss ball into trash can or until all cards are retrieved.

🏈 **What did you have to do to complete the drill?** (Watch. Imitate. Take a card.)

🏈 **When Andrew and Peter followed Jesus, what do you think they watched Jesus do? What things did they imitate?**

Conclusion: To be disciples of Jesus, we are to follow or imitate Him. Let's help each other think of ways we can follow or imitate Jesus today. Each team member moves to the station (see *Strategy Stations* activity on next page) indicated by the letter on his or her index card.

© 2004 Gospel Light. Permission to photocopy granted. *Raising Up Spiritual Champions*

2. Strategy Stations

Materials: Strategy Stations (pp. 65-66), scissors, masking tape, eight large sheets of colored construction paper, markers; optional—*Champions Music* CD and player.

Preparation: Photocopy and cut Strategy Stations pages apart and tape one section to each of the sheets of construction paper. Lay prepared sheets around a table or tape to walls in word order.)

Procedure: Each team member completes the sentence starter on the Strategy Station poster by which he or she is standing. **Complete the sentence by telling something about what it means to follow Jesus today.** After several minutes, signal time and invite team members to move to different stations. Continue as time permits or until each team member has completed each sentence starter. (Optional: Play "I Want to Follow Jesus" from *Champions Music* CD as team members work.)

When team members have completed writing, read aloud and review some of the responses to the sentence starters. (Note: Posters will be used later in the session.)

Conclusion: We've listed some good examples of ways to be disciples of Jesus. Now you can think about what you want to do to show that you want to be a follower and imitator of Jesus.

3. Playbook Preparation

Materials: *Session 1 Student Page* (pp. 67-68) for each team member, Strategy Stations posters, pencils.

Procedure: Distribute *Student Pages* and pencils to team members. Using the Strategy Stations posters for reference, each team member selects a phrase to copy onto his or her *Student Page* beside each letter of the word "disciple."

Optional: Make Playbooks!

Provide a paper or vinyl binder for each team member to use throughout **Raising Up Spiritual Champions.** Before Session 1, photocopy and place *Session 1 Student Page* in each binder. Provide materials (markers, gel pens, stickers, etc.) for team members to use in decorating and personalizing their playbooks. If binders have a front cover pocket, reproduce one of the logos on page 185 to slide into binder covers. Students take binders home after each session to complete at-home assignments. During session, team members insert the appropriate *Student Page.*

© 2004 Gospel Light. Permission to photocopy granted. *Raising Up Spiritual Champions*

RALLY (10-20 minutes)

Materials: *Champions Music* CD and player, each team member's *Session 1 Student Page*, *Session 1 Parent Page* (pp. 69-70) for each team member, pencils.

Worship: To signal team members to gather, play "I Want to Follow Jesus" from *Champions Music* CD. Invite team members to sing "I Want to Follow Jesus." **One of the ways people show they are disciples of Jesus is by worshiping Him. What are ways people worship Jesus?** (Sing. Pray. Tell about God's goodness.) Sing "I Want to Follow Jesus" again.

Another part of our training to be disciples is to learn to pray for each other. Share a prayer request or reason to praise God and then invite team members to share prayer requests or praises. Pray together, inviting volunteers to say sentence prayers as time and interest allow. Close the prayer time, asking God to help each team member follow Jesus. Be sensitive to how comfortable team members feel praying aloud. Structure your prayer time so that no team member feels pressured to participate. (Optional: Coaches lead groups of 8 to 12 team members in prayer time. You may also choose to keep a record of prayer requests, referring to the record each week during Rally time.)

Wrap-Up: Point out the activities on the *Student Page* that are to be done at home and those that require parent involvement. Invite questions about the first week's assignment. **Be sure your parents read the *Parent Pages*. They also need to help you complete each playbook page during the week and sign off in the boxes. At the next session, I will listen to you repeat the Bible verse you memorized and will also look at and sign off on the completed page. Players who complete every week's page will get a special MVP award at the end of the season! When we're training, it's wise to get the help we need. Our goal is to help each other become the best disciples we can be!** Point out your phone number and e-mail address on the *Parent Page*.

Be sure every team member leaves with his or her *Student Page* and *Parent Page*.

Give Me a "D"!

Invent a cheer using the letters of the word "disciple." It can be as simple as "Give me a 'D'! Give me an 'I'!" and so on. Or challenge team members to add a descriptive line that begins with that letter of the word ("D—Doin' what's right, every day!", "I—I follow Jesus, 'cause He is the way!" and so on).

Parent Connections

Parents are an integral part of **Raising Up Spiritual Champions**. There are weekly assignments on the *Student Pages* that involve parent interaction. In addition, the *Parent Pages* found with each session are meant to be reproduced and sent home weekly as a way to help parents think about their significant role in discipling their children. If a child's parents are unable to provide help, meet with the child yourself or arrange for another adult to meet with the child.

RELATIONSHIP is what it's all about!

Use every moment of the session to build relationships! During times when team members are gathering or waiting, ask open-ended questions. **Where do you like to go for fun? What books have you read recently? What's your favorite sport? What food do you like best? What videos do you enjoy? What's your easiest subject in school? Hardest subject?**

© 2004 Gospel Light. Permission to photocopy granted. *Raising Up Spiritual Champions*

LET ME TELL YOU

Based on John 1:35-49

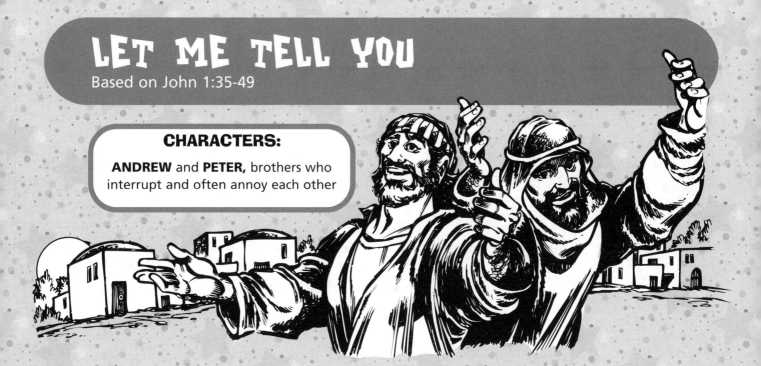

CHARACTERS:

ANDREW and **PETER,** brothers who interrupt and often annoy each other

(To audience.) I'm Andrew and this is my brother Peter. We're here—

(Interrupting.) to tell you some of the reasons we followed Jesus!

And a lot about the NAMES people called Him.

And what about the name He gave ME? *(To Andrew.)* But this is YOUR part of the story. Take it away, Andrew!

My friend John and I had gone to hear John the Baptist preach. There were huge crowds of people—

(Interrupting.) John the Baptist was the biggest thing to hit Israel in a LONG time. EVERYONE wanted to hear what he had to say!

© 2004 Gospel Light. Permission to photocopy granted. *Raising Up Spiritual Champions*

ANDREW (Looks at Peter, annoyed.) Now back to MY STORY! We were talking with John the Baptist. All of a sudden, he stopped talking, pointed to someone who was walking nearby and said, "LOOK! It's the Lamb of God who takes away the sin of the WORLD!"

PETER WOW! Strange name—Lamb of God. And the man John the Baptist was pointing to was a rabbi by the name of Jesus! Andrew and his friend didn't know what to think!

ANDREW John the Baptist had been telling us to get ready for the Messiah—the One God had promised to send. But John didn't say Jesus was the Messiah. He said He was the LAMB of GOD! It was SO confusing! We HAD to find out what he meant!

PETER My brother and his friend didn't have the nerve to ask Jesus straight out who He was. So they tried just following Him around. But Jesus knew what they were up to. He just turned around and asked them what they wanted!

ANDREW I guess we were pretty obvious. I felt kind of silly. After all, what can you say? "You're the LAMB OF GOD?! COOL! Can I have Your autograph?" Nah! So I asked, "Uh . . . where are You staying?" It was all I could think of!

PETER Kind of a lame question, but Jesus was kind. He invited them to come with Him.

ANDREW (To Peter.) Hey. This is MY part of the story, OK? (To audience.) We stayed with Jesus all day long. We listened to everything He said. And as we listened, we realized that whatever that Lamb of God name meant, Jesus WAS the Messiah! I had to tell Peter!

PETER And he did! He RAN up to me panting, "We have found the MESSIAH!" I said, "HOLD ON! WHAT are you talking about?"

ANDREW I didn't waste my breath explaining! Nope! I just dragged him off to meet Jesus for himself!

© 2004 Gospel Light. Permission to photocopy granted. *Raising Up Spiritual Champions*

PETER And what a meeting! Jesus didn't shake my hand. He didn't say, "Nice to meet you."

ANDREW No. He just LOOKED at you. (*To audience*.) Then guess what He said?

PETER Jesus said, "You're Simon, Jonas's son. I'm going to call you PETER!"

ANDREW Some nickname, huh? "Rock!" (*Lightly taps* Peter's *head.*)

PETER How could He give me a nickname? He didn't even KNOW ME! (*Pauses, thinking.*) I guess that was the point. He was telling me He DID know me already!

ANDREW We weren't the only ones who started following Jesus. Our friend Philip met Jesus the next day. After Phil had hung around and listened to Jesus for a while, he realized that Jesus was the Messiah, too! So he ran and found his buddy Nathanael, just like I had done with Peter. He told Nate, "We've found the One Moses and all the prophets wrote about! It's Jesus of Nazareth!"

PETER But Nate wasn't impressed at all! He snorted, "Nazareth! Can ANYTHING good come from THERE?"

ANDREW Nate thought Jesus' hometown was kind of a dump. But Philip dragged Nate off to meet Jesus, too! When Jesus saw Nate coming, He did something odd, again.

PETER He looked at Nate and said, "Here is a true Israelite indeed."

ANDREW Nate was amazed. "How do You know me?" Nate asked.

PETER Jesus told Nate that He'd seen him under the fig tree before Philip had ever talked with him. Well, Nate may have thought Nazareth was a dump, but he was sure impressed with JESUS! Nate said to Jesus, "You are the Son of God! YOU are the King of Israel!"

ANDREW Now for part two. We went back home and we were fishing as usual.

PETER But we weren't THINKING as usual. Jesus had given us a LOT of new stuff to think about.

ANDREW One day, Peter and I were hip deep in water, tossing our nets. We heard someone calling to us and looked up. Jesus was on the shore!

PETER I'll never forget what He said. "Follow Me, and I will make you fishers of men."

ANDREW We'd been talking about Jesus ever since we'd come back home. But now Jesus wanted us to *follow* Him. Jesus wanted us to come with Him, listen to Him and do whatever He did!

PETER We really didn't know what we were getting into. Fishing for people, not fish?! More strange ideas! But we dropped our nets anyway and followed Him then!

ANDREW My buddy John, who had also met Jesus before, was mending nets with his brother James and their dad. John must have told his dad and brother all about Jesus because when Jesus called to them, they gave their nets to their dad and followed Jesus, too!

PETER After that, we spent every day with Jesus. We watched Him. We listened to Him. We tried to remember everything He said and imitate everything He did!

ANDREW And that's how we became Jesus' disciples!

© 2004 Gospel Light. Permission to photocopy granted. *Raising Up Spiritual Champions*

STRATEGY STATIONS

Deciding to follow Jesus means . . .

If I follow Jesus, He will . . .

Something that might help me to be Jesus' disciple is . . .

Choosing to follow Jesus means I might need to . . .

© 2004 Gospel Light. Permission to photocopy granted. *Raising Up Spiritual Champions*

If I could take one step to follow Jesus, it would be . . . .

Please help me, God, to . . . .

Living like Jesus means . . . .

Every day I can follow Jesus by . . . .

© 2004 Gospel Light. Permission to photocopy granted. *Raising Up Spiritual Champions*

The Write Stuff

Look at each completed Strategy Stations poster. Copy your favorite answer from each poster near the corresponding letter.

© 2004 Gospel Light. Permission to photocopy granted. *Raising Up Spiritual Champions*

THE CHALLENGE

This session's Bible Memory Verse:

"Just as you received Christ Jesus as Lord, continue to live in him, rooted and built up in him, strengthened in the faith as you were taught, and overflowing with thankfulness."
Colossians 2:6-7

Bible Memory
Verse repeated.
Coach's initials

Session 1
page completed.
Coach's initials

Read Colossians 2:6-7.

What images come to mind when you think of something being rooted or built? On another sheet of paper (or on your computer), draw two pictures that help you think about what this session's Bible memory verse means. Tell a friend or family member about each drawing.

Did it!
Parent's initials

Family Challenge

Plant seeds or a small plant. Watch the growth!

Talk About: What do followers of Jesus need to grow as disciples?

Imagination Questions: Is reading God's Word more like rain, like sunshine or like good things in the soil? Why do you think so? How do you think prayer can help us grow? How does being with God's family, the Church, help us grow?

Did it!
Parent's initials

Choose one of

the answers you wrote beside a letter of the word "disciple." Think about what action you could do this week to help a friend or family member understand your answer and what it means. Then do it!

Did it!
Parent's initials

 © 2004 Gospel Light. Permission to photocopy granted. *Raising Up Spiritual Champions*

What Does It Mean to Be a Disciple?

For more information about this week's question, read Mark 1:14-20 and John 1:35-49, the sources for our Bible study. You may also read Ephesians 4:20—5:10; Philippians 2:1-16.

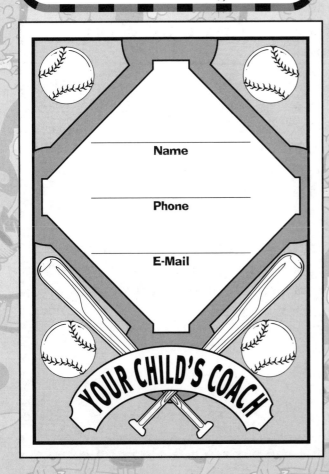

Name

Phone

E-Mail

YOUR CHILD'S COACH

Discipleship Every Day

In Deuteronomy 6:7, God commanded parents to teach their children about Him "when you sit at home and when you walk along the road, when you lie down and when you get up." The most important learning in life takes place not in churches, schools or scout troops but in families. The hours and days we spend together simply living through what seem to be routine activities are the prime opportunities for building spiritual foundations!

Every parent teaches his or her children about God every moment they are together—even parents who are nonbelievers! What we truly believe comes through loud and clear to our children through our daily actions and responses to life's little surprises. Every contact we have with our kids or with others in our kids' presence shows not only what we know or don't know about God's Word but also whether we believe those things enough to live by them. God will enable us to use these everyday moments to their fullest potential as we trust and ask Him!

Here are some simple ways to incorporate following Jesus into our daily lives:

"When you sit at home"

❖ Have an established dinnertime and sit together at meals. (Did you know that having dinner together is the single most accurate predictor of a child's academic success?) When you are together, don't

© 2004 Gospel Light. Permission to photocopy granted. *Raising Up Spiritual Champions*

talk over the kids; talk *with* them. Include even the youngest in the conversation. Ask "what do you think?" kinds of questions to keep everyone engaged. Show the manners you expect instead of nagging.

🍂 Link God to your child's daily life in a way that has meaning for him or her. When your child reports having had a terrible day, listen and be sympathetic. But rather than a weak, "I'm sure things will be better tomorrow," try saying, "Wow! It sounds like you had a hard day. I'm glad God is with us on days like that. Let's pray right now that tomorrow will be better for you!"

"When you walk along the road"

🍂 As you travel in the car or take a walk, engage your kids in a game in which you see and name things God made. Increase the challenge by naming things in alphabetical order, naming things that rhyme or things that begin with the same sound.

🍂 Revel in the available natural wonders. Take your kids to the great outdoors, plant something together or go to an aquarium—looking at what God has made creates opportunities to share your sense of awe at God's creation! "God made these hummingbird eggs so perfect! And God loves us even more than He loves birds!"

"When you lie down"

🍂 Keep a consistent bedtime routine.

Plan time for your routine so that your kids (and you!) have time to unwind, relax and be ready to rest.

🍂 Make reading a Bible story or short devotional a regular part of your routine. (Books abound that are appropriate for every child's age level.) And don't forget that older kids still love listening as you read aloud a chapter of a longer story. Take time to thank God for the good things He has provided during the day and His care at night. It all adds up to relaxed kids and parents with minds focused on God and ready to rest.

"When you get up"

🍂 Make getting up something everyone likes to do! If you consistently go to bed early enough, this won't feel impossible. Study your children to see what can be done in the morning to help and motivate them. (Some need their clothes laid out ahead of time, for instance.)

🍂 Begin the morning by inviting God to be the center of your family's day. Take time to eat together, to look at, laugh with and enjoy each other. Ask God's care for your children as they leave for school.

🍂 Discover the luxury of not being rushed. (Try getting up 30 minutes earlier than usual each morning for a week!) Extra time can make morning a whole new experience!

© 2004 Gospel Light. Permission to photocopy granted. *Raising Up Spiritual Champions*

What Is Most Important to Me?

2 Session

The Coach's Corner

Researcher George Barna reports that by the age of 13, a person has formed his or her basic spiritual identity.[1] We recognize, however, that many preteens do not have a Christian identity nor do they base their decisions on biblical truth.

But rather than cause panic, such information should drive us to take stock of our own priorities! We've committed to help coach young believers toward becoming disciples of Christ. If our choices indeed reveal what is important to us, what will the kids with whom we interact learn from our choices? It is only when our *words* about God and His priorities are backed by our consistent *actions* that the words themselves become believable!

For instance, if we say we choose to seek God's kingdom as our first priority, how will our choice affect our time? Commitment to regular prayer and Bible study—before anything else—requires a daily choice. And choosing daily to take time to "seek first" God's kingdom is something for which we likely won't be paid or applauded! No one may ever know the details of our personal time with God, but our choice to consistently seek Him will transform our thoughts, our words and our actions. And when we focus our hearts daily on God first, Jesus said that everything else (that's *everything*!) will be given to us!

Take time this week to consider what it means for you to seek God's kingdom first. Be bold enough to invite God's Spirit to reveal your true priorities. Recognize which of your choices reveal a part of your life where God is not first in priority. Then ask Him to help you change your priorities where it's needed and to choose actions that will show Him—and you—that He is first in your life.

Note
1. George Barna, *Transforming Children into Spiritual Champions* (Ventura, CA: Regal Books, 2003), p. 34.

BIBLE MEMORY VERSE

"Seek first his kingdom and his righteousness, and all these things will be given to you as well." Matthew 6:33

Scripture Study
Luke 10:38-42

Aims:

1. To identify that Mary's choice to be with Jesus showed what was most important to her

2. To discuss how our choices reveal our priorities

3. To plan ways to put God first this week

© 2004 Gospel Light. Permission to photocopy granted. *Raising Up Spiritual Champions*

Session Game Plan

WARM-UP (10-20 minutes)

Materials: Large sheet of butcher paper, masking tape, marker, 10-15 household items in a bag.

Procedure: Play a game in which team members choose an item and tell why they chose it, and then discuss what people value and their reasons.

POWER-UP (20-30 minutes)

Materials: Bible for each team member.

Procedure: Read aloud a Bible passage, ask questions to determine how two people's choices revealed their priorities and then discuss or role-play other possible endings for the story.

PRACTICE (20-30 minutes)

Materials: *Session 2 Student Page* (pp. 79-80) for each team member; baseball bat, sheet of butcher paper and marker for each group of four to eight team members; Choices=Priorities poster from Warm-Up; pencils.

Procedure: Team members brainstorm situations and characters, playing a game to determine who answers. Team members may then act out role-plays that demonstrate what they learned. Each team member then completes a part of his or her *Student Page*.

RALLY (10-20 minutes)

Materials: *Champions Music* CD and player, each team member's *Session 2 Student Page, Session 2 Parent Page* (pp. 81-82) for each team member, pencils.

Procedure: Sing worship songs, talk about the week's assignment and pray together.

A TEAM OF THEIR OWN

Keep team spirit on the rise and help build relationships with and among team members in this fun way! Brainstorm a team name (anything from biblical names such as Peter's Power Team, Thomas's Titans, Daring Disciples to an adaptation of a popular sports team name), choose team colors, a team mascot and create a team cheer! If your team members are interested in developing cheers or raps, invite pairs or trios to set up a time outside of the session to create and practice the cheers or raps. Cheers or raps may communicate team names or ideas team members are discovering in **Raising Up Spiritual Champions.** Invite team members to demonstrate their cheers or raps during Rally time in any of the sessions or as part of the celebration in Session 8.

When cheers or raps are demonstrated, give a small prize to each team for a variety of noncompetitive categories such as Who cheers the loudest? Whose cheer has the best words? Which cheer is the hardest to say? Which cheer has the hardest motions? Who can do their cheer the most quietly? Whose cheer was funniest? Who added the most interesting uniforms or costumes?

© 2004 Gospel Light. Permission to photocopy granted. *Raising Up Spiritual Champions*

WARM-UP (10-20 minutes)

Materials: Large sheet of butcher paper, masking tape, 10-15 house-hold items (baseball, CD, eggbeater, toothbrush, money, etc.), marker.

Preparation: Tape butcher paper to wall. Set out house-hold items on a table.

Survivor's Choice

Procedure: We're going to take the Desert Island Challenge! Team members form pairs. **Find someone wearing the same color (shirt) as you are wearing. With your partner, look at the items on the table. Decide which one or two items you would choose to take with you to help you survive on a desert island. After you've decided, each pair will take a turn to tell what they chose and why.** Pairs discuss, decide and then take turns telling the reasons for selecting items. To help pairs think about what to choose, ask:

◆ **What things would you need in order to survive on a desert island?**

◆ **What kinds of tools could help you survive? What item here might be a good substitute for that tool?**

◆ **How many other ways could you use this item?**

◆ Hold up any two items. **Which of these two items do you think would be more valuable on a desert island? Why?**

◆ **How would you choose differently if you were (stranded in the middle of the woods) instead?**

After all pairs have shared their items and reasons say, **In our game, we based our choices on one priority: the need to survive.**

◆ **How did the item you chose help us know what part of survival you think is most important?** (Food. Water. Shelter. Safety. Signaling for help.)

If you're on a desert island, survival is the most important thing. Survival is your priority and was the basis for how we chose what was important in this activity. **As we think about what we do every day, however, our priorities and choices are different. Let's talk about some of the items we use every day.**

◆ Point to an item on the table. **What makes this (eggbeater) valuable in daily life?** Volunteers describe the use of items.

◆ **How does using a (toothbrush) every day reveal a person's priorities or show what a person thinks is important?** (Using a toothbrush daily may show we think having healthy teeth or avoiding going to the dentist or not having bad breath is important.)

Move to the paper taped to the wall. Write team members' answers to the following questions randomly on the paper, leaving an open area at the top of the paper. (Note: This poster will be used later in the session.)

◆ **What things do kids your age say are important?** (Wearing the right clothes. Family. Being with friends. Getting good grades. Playing sports. Video games.)

◆ **Why do you think a kid your age might say (friends) are important? Why do people say these things are a priority? Why is (playing video games) a priority?** Add reasons below each item written on the paper. **What we choose reveals our priorities or what we think is most important.**

Conclusion: What we choose every day shows what is important to us, no matter what we might say is important. Our priorities—the things we put first—are shown by what we choose to do! Write across the top of the paper: CHOICES=PRIORITIES

POWER-UP (20-30 minutes)

Materials: Bible for each team member.

KEEP YOUR BRAINSTORMING POSTERS

The butcher paper lists and charts made during each class session are valuable records of your team members' thought processes and will be used again during Sessions 7 and 8. Keep posters on the walls, adding new ones each week. If this is not possible, consider using poster board or other sturdy material for longer-lasting posters that will be easy to display and remove.

Procedure: Be sure each team member has a Bible. **Let's find Luke chapter 10, verse 38. We're going to read this short story out loud and see what we can discover about the choices and priorities of two people.** Designate one reader or invite volunteers to take turns reading the passage. After reading the passage, ask the following questions:

☺ **What did Mary choose to do?** (In verse 39, Mary sat at the Lord's feet and listened to what He said.)

☺ **What else could Mary have chosen to do?** (Worked. Cooked.)

☺ **What did her actions show?** (That she thought being with Jesus was more important than preparing food.)

☺ **What did Jesus say about these choices?** (In verse 41, Jesus said that Martha was worried and upset. In verse 42, Jesus said that Mary chose what is better.)

☺ **What do you think Martha might have done after this account ends?**

☺ **Who are you most like in the story? Who are most kids like?**

After team members talk about the story, invite pairs formed during Survivor's Choice to join each other again. Ask the following questions:

☺ **How could the story have ended differently?**

Pairs consult and think of one way in which this story might have ended differently and then act out or simply tell their ideas.

☺ **Why do you think Jesus said Mary had "chosen what is better"?** (In verse 42, Jesus said that what she had chosen could not be taken away from her.)

☺ **What would this story be like if it happened today?**

☺ **What do you think Jesus meant when He said "only one thing is needed"?**

☺ **Read Matthew 6:33. How do you think Jesus' words in this verse help you understand what Jesus meant by "only one thing is needed?"**

Jesus says we are to seek God's kingdom first. That means we need to make paying attention to Him our top priority! It's what

© 2004 Gospel Light. Permission to photocopy granted. *Raising Up Spiritual Champions*

Mary was doing when she dropped everything to choose to spend time with Jesus. Was Jesus saying that work and food aren't important? No, obviously they are very necessary, but being with Him is even more important.

Conclusion: God wants us to put Him first in the way we think, what we do and what we say. When we choose to put God first, we are showing that getting to know God and showing our love for Him are priorities in our lives. The first step in getting to know God is becoming a member of God's family. If you have questions about doing that, I'd like to talk with you. If any team member indicates interest in becoming a member of God's family, arrange a time to talk (see "Leading a Student to Christ" on p. 39).

Two women may dress in Bible-times costumes to act as Martha and Mary, pantomiming possible actions by Martha (preparing and serving food, cleaning house, etc.) and Mary (sitting down to listen to Jesus) as the passage is read aloud. After the passage is read, allow team members to ask actors questions about the incident.

© 2004 Gospel Light. Permission to photocopy granted. *Raising Up Spiritual Champions*

PRACTICE (20-30 minutes)

Materials: Baseball bat, sheet of butcher paper prepared as shown and marker for each group of four to eight team members; optional—bite-sized snack.

1. Bat Grab

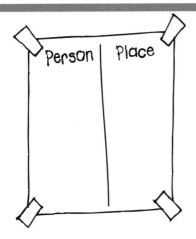

Person | Place

Procedure: To help us get ready to play a game about putting God first in our lives, we're going to have a contest to fill in the columns on this poster. The winner of each bat grab may name a person. To play bat grab: Two to four team members at a time quickly place hands around the bat, filling in the space up to the top (see sketch). Team member who grabs bat last is the winner and tells a word ("friend," "dad," "teacher," "soccer coach," etc.) to be written in the first column. (Optional: Winner receives bite-sized snack.) Repeat activity several times and then continue with the other category, challenging players to add as many places (school, mall, friend's house, etc.) as possible in a short time.

Now for the next challenge: According to Matthew 6:33, God wants us to put Him first and make Him the priority in what we choose to think, what we choose to do and what we choose to say! A good way to do that is to ask these two questions: What can I do to show

love for God in this situation? and What can I do to show love for others in this situation?

We're going to play the bat grab game again. The winner will choose a word from each category on our poster to create a sentence that tells a way in which the person in that setting could show he or she puts God first by showing love for God or others. Play bat grab several more times, allowing winners to create sentences ("When you and your friend are at school, you can be friendly to others." "When your dad asks you a question at home, you can be honest with him.") If needed, invite person who wins the bat grab to select a teammate with whom to consult or to select another teammate to answer.

© 2004 Gospel Light. Permission to photocopy granted. *Raising Up Spiritual Champions*

Now, with your partner from the Survivor's Choice activity, choose one of the sentences we just heard and use it as the story line for a role-play you can do with your partner. Invite as many pairs to role-play situations as time and interest allow. Help team members with their role-plays by asking questions such as **What should happen first in your role-play? What will happen next? How might your role-play end?** (Optional: Instead of role-plays, pairs may simply describe situations.)

Conclusion: We've been talking a lot about how the things we do and say every day show what is most important to us. Some of the things we choose don't really make much difference—like whether we choose to eat an apple or an orange. Other choices can make a big difference in our lives and the lives of our friends and family. For example, if we choose to be honest, our friends and families learn they can trust us. Our choices can either help or hurt others. Keep in mind that loving God and others will help us make choices to show that being a disciple of Jesus is the most important thing to us.

GO FOR THE GOAL!

The **goal** of this activity is to give team members a chance to show how to put God first by choosing to act in ways that show love for God for others.

2. Playbook Preparation

Materials: *Session 2 Student Page* (pp. 79-80) for each team member, Choices=Priorities poster from Warm-Up, pencils.

Procedure: Distribute *Student Pages* and pencils to team members. Team members complete "The Write Stuff" section. **Each of you will have answers that are unique to you, but be sure to talk with your coaches and with each other about your answers.**

Check-Off Time: Team members who completed *Session 1 Student Pages* may show their completed pages to you and recite the previous session's Bible Memory Verse during this time. As time permits, ask questions about the at-home assignments: **What part did you enjoy? What was hard to do? Remember to bring back your completed page from each previous session. I'll look it over and then sign off in the boxes. Players who complete every session's page will get a special MVP award at the end of the season!**

Optional: Keeping Up with the Playbooks!

Keep a hole punch available for your team members to insert their new pages into their playbooks. Extend the Playbook Preparation time for those who have not yet completed decorating their playbooks.

RALLY (10-20 minutes)

Materials: *Champions Music* CD and player, each team member's *Session 2 Student Page, Session 2 Parent Page* for each team member (pp. 81-82), pencils.

Worship: To signal Rally time play "I Want to Follow Jesus" from *Champions Music* CD and, after team members gather, sing the song together. If time permits, invite volunteer pairs who acted out a role-play earlier to repeat one or more of the role-plays as time and interest allow.

Part of our training in learning how to be disciples of Jesus is to learn to pray for each other. Share a prayer request or reason to praise God and then invite team members to share praises and prayer requests. Invite volunteers to complete the following prayer starter aloud or silently: "Dear God, please help me to put You first this week by . . ." Close the prayer time by thanking God for His help and care. (Optional: Coaches lead groups of 8 to 12 team members in prayer time. If you started a record of prayer requests during Session 1, refer to it during this prayer time.)

Wrap-Up: Take time to invite questions about the second side of the *Session 2 Student Page.* Be sure every team member leaves with his or her playbook or *Student Page* as well as a *Parent Page*.

© 2004 Gospel Light. Permission to photocopy granted. *Raising Up Spiritual Champions*

What Is Most Important to Me?

1ST PLACE

The Write Stuff

Look at the poster that says "CHOICES=PRIORITIES."

Choose a priority listed there. Then draw and/or write a scene about YOU and the priority you chose and how you can put God first.

As you write or draw, remember to answer these questions!
1. When I (fill in the priority), what is a way to show I love God?
2. When I (fill in the priority), what is a way to show I love others?
Show and explain your finished scene to a friend or coach.

© 2004 Gospel Light. Permission to photocopy granted. *Raising Up Spiritual Champions*

THE CHALLENGE

This session's Bible Memory Verse:

"Seek first his kingdom and his righteousness, and all these things will be given to you as well." Matthew 6:33

Bible Memory Verse repeated.
Coach's initials

Session 2 page completed.
Coach's initials

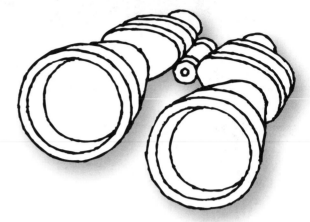

Pantomime for a friend

or family member an activity you enjoy very much. When the person guesses the activity correctly, ask that person to tell one way you could put God first while you do that activity. (Look at the two questions on the other side of this page for help!)

Did it!
Parent's initials

On another sheet of paper,
draw a circle.

Divide the circle into four sections.

Label the sections "morning," "afternoon," "evening" and "weekend." In each section, write a way you could put God first during that time.

Did it!
Parent's initials

Family Challenge

Play Hot or Cold!—with a twist! One person closes his or her eyes. Another person hides an object. The person with closed eyes begins to look for the object, keeping his or her eyes closed. The hider tells the seeker he or she is "hot" if moving near the object and "cold" if moving away from the object. Repeat until everyone has had a turn to be the seeker.

Talk About: What helped you find the object? What made it difficult? How did you feel when you were "hot"? When you heard you were "cold"?

Imagination Questions: Read Matthew 6:33. If you were a knight in ancient times, how would you find a kingdom you were seeking? Who might be able to help you? What is a way we can show we are in God's kingdom (loving God and others) today in our own family?

Did it!
Parent's initials

© 2004 Gospel Light. Permission to photocopy granted. *Raising Up Spiritual Champions*

What Is Most Important to Me?

For more information about this week's question, read Luke 10:38-42, the source for our Bible study. You may also read Matthew 6:25-34.

Bible Study with Children

Children (and all of us) have an innate love for a good story. That must be one of the reasons God wrote so many good stories into His Word! But as children mature, the Bible can move beyond the level of a storybook to become a source of exciting information and motivation that has great meaning for a child's own life.

While there are a host of devotional products available for parents to buy, let's look at effective ways to help our children learn to read and understand God's Word itself. What can a parent do to help a child learn how to study and understand the Bible on his or her own?

Consider the following points in choosing what to study together:

First, examine your own experience. What parts of the Bible did you understand best when you first began reading? What parts do you like best to read now? (If you're not a Bible reader, take this opportunity to discover God's Word with your child!) Mark's Gospel is a great book to start reading together.

Second, choose a topic, book or portion to study that closely connects with your child's own life and challenges. Let your child know that you're going to look together into God's Word for answers about his or her situation!

Is your child being bullied at school? Try studying David's life together.

Does your child have a hard time with peer pressure? Daniel is a great example of integrity.

Is your daughter consumed with the way she looks? Look at Esther to see how a woman who had external beauty became a woman of internal beauty and courage.

The goal is to help your child see that God's Word is not just a history book or a

© 2004 Gospel Light. Permission to photocopy granted. *Raising Up Spiritual Champions*

book of rules but God's instructions for how to have successful, joyful lives. The more your child comes to know God through His Word, the more God equips him or her to deal positively with the problems of modern life. To lecture a child about the evils to avoid (drugs, sex, drinking) without introducing him or her to the God who fills their deepest longings and gives them the power to resist temptation is a great disservice to any child.

Consider these questions as you read a short passage together. Choose to talk about one or two of these questions as you read together:

☺ What are the keywords and phrases of this passage?

☺ How would you put these keywords and phrases in your own words?

☺ What does God say about Himself in this passage?

☺ What does God say about people in general in this passage?

☺ What does God say about me in this passage?

☺ Does this passage tell something I should do? Should avoid doing?

☺ How would I explain this passage to a younger child?

Your excitement, involvement and honest application of what you read to your own life will teach your child more about studying God's Word than any devotional book or study guide ever could do! Because the Bible is true, its people are real and God is at work in our lives just as He was in theirs, reading the Bible thoughtfully together can become your family's finest adventure!

© 2004 Gospel Light. Permission to photocopy granted. *Raising Up Spiritual Champions*

How Does Knowing the Truth Make a Difference in My Life?

The Coach's Corner

The Barna Research Group lists seven basic questions whose answers determine one's worldview.[1] The final question of the seven echoes the words of Pontius Pilate: "What is truth?" As in Pilate's day, current thinking largely denies that truth is knowable, absolute or unchanging. But without truth, morals are up for grabs and character doesn't count.

Even in Christian circles, we may find that truth is not always known or practiced! Without putting God's truth into our lives by regular, prayerful reading and thinking, we may hit the highlights but never get a grasp of the "whole counsel of God," as it was called in days gone by. Psalm 25:4-5 points out that learning God's Word and His truth is not the product of a few quick overviews. It is a daily process that begins with seeing ("show me") and continues with learning ("teach me") and then walking—living out what is taught ("guide me"): This is the core of understanding God's truth in a way that goes beyond informing our heads to changing our hearts and our lives!

Take the Psalm 25:4-5 challenge this week! Read the same Scripture passage daily for a week. Grab a notebook and create three categories in which you write every day: "What does this show me? What does it teach me? What will I do so that God can guide me (to apply it) as I walk through this week?" Write in a journal throughout the week to see how God will open your mind and heart to truth that not only instructs but transforms as well!

Note
1. George Barna, *Transforming Children into Spiritual Champions* (Ventura, CA: Regal Books, 2003), p. 70.

BIBLE MEMORY VERSE

"Show me your ways, O Lord, teach me your paths; guide me in your truth and teach me, for you are God my Savior, and my hope is in you all day long." Psalm 25:4-5

Scripture Study

James 1:22-27; 3:1-3

Aims:

1. To discover that God's Word is like a mirror that shows us truth about ourselves

2. To use God's Word to evaluate our words and actions

3. To practice ways to put God's truth into action every day

Session Game Plan

WARM-UP (10-20 minutes)

Materials: Large sheet of butcher paper, masking tape, marker.

Procedure: Play a game in which team members tell true and false statements about themselves to discuss reasons we think something is true. Brainstorm and discuss sources of truth.

POWER-UP (20-30 minutes)

Materials: Bible; a variety of items that give a reflection (spoon, shiny bowl, piece of aluminum foil, etc.), including a hand mirror; several dot stickers; pencil and paper for each team member.

Procedure: Explore the importance and purpose of a true reflection and then read, discuss and illustrate a Bible passage. Use dot stickers to illustrate the action of the Bible passage.

PRACTICE (20-30 minutes)

Materials: Bible; *Session 3 Student Page* (pp. 93-94) for each team member; What's My Question? (pp. 91-92); scissors; masking tape; large sheet of construction paper for each pair or trio of team members; hand mirrors; each team member's pictures-and-question page from Power-Up; markers; pencils.

Procedure: Team members form pairs or trios and then use mirrors to decipher Scripture references, discuss Scripture and write questions backwards (or forwards) that help them apply what they read. Team members may use mirrors to complete part of *Session 3 Student Page*.

RALLY (10-20 minutes)

Materials: *Champions Music* CD and player, each team member's *Session 3 Student Page*, *Session 3 Parent Page* (pp. 95-96) for each team member, pencils.

Procedure: Sing worship songs, talk about the week's assignment and pray together.

Introducing the Amazing Itty-Bitty Spiritual Exercise Journal

The Amazing Itty-Bitty Spiritual Exercise Journal will be introduced to team members in Session 5. However, to help your team members get into shape a little earlier, consider preparing a copy of the Amazing Itty-Bitty Spiritual Exercise Journal (pp. 127-128) for each team member to use during this week (along with the *Session 3 Student Page*). Encourage team members to use the journal instead of blank paper as they learn the "show me, lead me, teach me, guide me" method of Bible study discussed on the *Student Page*.

© 2004 Gospel Light. Permission to photocopy granted. *Raising Up Spiritual Champions*

WARM-UP (10-20 minutes)

Two Truths and a Tale

Materials: Large sheet of paper, masking tape, marker.

Preparation: Tape paper to wall.

GO FOR THE GOAL!

Today's goal goes beyond convincing kids that God's Word is true. Our goal is to help kids understand how to allow God's truth to make a difference in their lives: by first recognizing the **value** of looking into God's Word daily, and then by finding and understanding God's **truth** and how they can **evaluate** their words and actions in light of that truth. They need to then **put truth into action** by changing their attitude to reflect what they discovered in God's Word. Changed attitudes lead to changed behaviors!

Procedure: Team members sit in a circle. (If group is large or time is limited, divide into several groups of no more than eight team members per group.) **We're going to play Two Truths and a Tale. Each of you may tell in any order two things about yourself that are true and something that is not true. We'll try to figure out which statement is not true!**

Begin by saying statements about yourself and then allow time for team members to think of their statements and then take turns saying statements aloud. After each team member makes three statements, others vote by raising hands on which statement they think is not true. Team member identifies the untrue statement. Volunteers tell why they voted as they did. (Optional: Team members write statements on index cards. Statements are read aloud by others so that correct responses are not accidentally given away.)

❧ **Why did you think it was not true that (Brittney has a rabbit)?** (She talks about her pet dog often but not about a rabbit.)

❧ **What made you think it was true that (Chad once ate six hamburgers)?** (He always eats more than anyone else.)

❧ **What helped you decide which statements were true or not true?** (Knowing what people are like; whether what they say matches their actions.)

One of the ways we decide if someone is telling the truth is to see if their actions match their words. **What are some other ways we find out the truth about everyday things?** Write responses on the prepared paper.

❧ **Which source would you trust to give you the true time of day: a friend or the clock? Why?**

❧ **What's the best way to find out how to get to a place you've never been: look on a map or ask for directions? Why?**

❧ **How can you find out the truth about (whether your hair is combed, whether your face is clean, whether you have spinach in your teeth)?** (Use a mirror.)

❧ **What are some jobs in which a person needs a mirror?** (Dentist. Hair stylist. Astronomer. Truck driver.) **How does a mirror help a person doing that job?**

❧ **What do you think will happen if a (truck driver) ignores what he or she sees in the mirror?**

Conclusion: There are lots of ways to get accurate information about some things. But when it comes to getting accurate information about what's right or wrong, God's Word is like a true mirror. It helps us see what we are really like and then shows us what we should be like. Let's do an experiment with some different ways to look at our reflections.

© 2004 Gospel Light. Permission to photocopy granted. *Raising Up Spiritual Champions*

POWER-UP (20-30 minutes)

Materials: Bible; a variety of items that give a reflection (spoon, shiny bowl, piece of aluminum foil, etc.), including a hand mirror; several dot stickers; pencil and paper for each team member.

Preparation: Set out the reflective items where team members may freely examine them. Just before this activity, place several dot stickers on your face or on the face of another adult.

SHINE SEEKERS!

As you talk with team members about mirrors and other shiny items that give a reflection, invite them to look around the room. **Who can find some other items in this room that give a reflection?** Invite team members to view and compare their reflections as seen in these items.

Procedure: What is the same about these items? (They each give back a reflection.) Team members view and compare the quality of reflections from different items.

⚽ **(Dena), describe how your reflection looks in the (foil).**

⚽ **(Wyatt), which of these items do you think gives the most accurate or truthful reflection? Which gives the least accurate reflection?**

☺ **How do you know which reflection is the best?** (We've seen true reflections in good mirrors before.)

☺ **What if you had never seen yourself in a good mirror before? How would you know if these other reflections were any good?**

Distribute Bibles, paper and pencils to team members. **Let's turn to a letter written by James, Jesus' brother. Find chapter 1, verse 22. We're going to use the paper and pencils to**

 © 2004 Gospel Light. Permission to photocopy granted. *Raising Up Spiritual Champions*

draw pictures or symbols to help us remember the ideas in this passage.

At some point, team members will let you know that you have stickers stuck to your face. **What do you mean, I have stickers on my face? How do I know you're telling me the truth?** Hold one of the reflective items to your face.

I can't really see what you're talking about. This reflection isn't very clear. Are you really telling me the truth?

Invite a team member to hold a mirror to your face. **Oh, I see. There are stickers on my (cheek and my nose). Thanks.** Turn away from the mirror but do not remove the stickers.

Invite volunteers to read James 1:22-24 aloud.

(Note: Pictures-and-question pages made by team members in this activity will be used later in the session.)

☻ **What picture or symbol could you draw to help you remember these words? My face would be a perfect illustration! I looked into the mirror. It gave me a true reflection. I saw clearly what was stuck to my face.**

☻ **What might be an example of a person who listens to the Word but does not do what it says?** (One who reads in the Bible that God says not to lie and then lies. Someone who knows God's Word says to be kind and then acts unkindly.)

So the Bible says that when we look into or listen to God's Word, it's like using a good mirror. We find out the truth. I couldn't tell the truth about my face without a good mirror. But if a person doesn't put God's truth into action, the person is like me with my messy face. I saw the truth. But seeing my face in a true mirror did not clean up my face, did it? What else needs to happen for my face to be clean?

Let's read verse 25.

☻ **How is this second man different?** (He looks intently. He pays attention. He doesn't forget what he heard. He does what he has heard.)

☻ **What picture or symbol could you draw to help you remember these words?**

Look into a mirror as you remove the stickers from your face. **Now I am going to be like the man in verse 25. I have a true reflection in front of me. I can see what I need to do. And I am going to do something about it! I am going to put the truth into action!**

God's Word is true. We can trust it to be like an accurate mirror. It tells us the truth about how we really are and how we should be. But James says that knowing what is true is not enough. We have to do something about the truth. First, we have to evaluate what we do and say by God's truth. Second, we need to act on what we know or put the truth into action. Otherwise, we're like the first man who forgot what he saw!

© 2004 Gospel Light. Permission to photocopy granted. *Raising Up Spiritual Champions*

Invite a volunteer to read James 1:26-27.

⚽ **What are ways James lists that we can put the truth into action?** (Keep a tight rein on the tongue. Care for people in need.)

⚽ **What could you draw to remind you of these three ways? Draw or write reminders of them.**

Let's focus on one of these ways: keeping a tight rein on our tongues. It's one of God's truths we can put into action all the time—unless we're sleeping!

⚽ **Which of you has ever ridden a horse?**

⚽ **When you pull back or tighten the horse's reins, what happens?** (The horse slows and stops. A little person now has control over a big horse.)

⚽ **What happens if you keep a tight rein on a horse as you ride?** (The horse won't go too fast. You will have control. The horse doesn't run away with you.)

⚽ **What do you think James means by keeping a tight rein on our tongues?** (Slow down. Stop our words.)

Invite a team member to read James 3:1-3.

⚽ **What shows that a person is perfect or complete? What does James say about a person who can control his or her words?** (A perfect or complete person is never at fault or wrong in what he says. If a person can control what he or she says, the person can control his or her whole body.)

⚽ **So when we have control over our words, it shows we know how to control** the rest of ourselves, too. Why do you think that is true? (Because it is so easy to say words we should not say.)

⚽ **What picture or symbol could you draw to help you remember these words?**

⚽ **What questions could we ask ourselves about our words before we say them?** (Will these words make people glad? Will these words hurt people or make them sad? Will I be sorry I said this later? Will these words be pleasing to God?) **When we ask ourselves these kinds of questions, it's like holding our words in front of the mirror. We are testing our ideas and words by God's truth!**

On your paper, write the question you think is the best one to ask. Repeat questions as needed.

Conclusion: We've heard some good truth from God's Word. We've thought of some good questions to ask about the words we say. Now we're going to practice evaluating other parts of our lives by using God's Word.

© 2004 Gospel Light. Permission to photocopy granted. *Raising Up Spiritual Champions*

PRACTICE (20-30 minutes)

1. Message Discoveries

Materials: Bible; What's My Question? (pp. 91-92); scissors; masking tape; large sheet of construction paper for each pair or trio of team members; hand mirrors; each team member's pictures-and-question page from Power-Up; markers.

Preparation: Photocopy What's My Question? pages and cut apart into sections. Tape each section to the top of a sheet of construction paper, making one paper for each pair or trio of team members. Tape papers to wall at team members' eye level (see sketch). (Note: Posters will be used later in the session.)

Procedure: Let's form pairs or trios for our practice time. If you're wearing blue, find one or two other people who are wearing blue. Continue using other characteristics (brown eyes, color or style of shoes, etc.) until everyone is in a pair or trio.

Be sure each pair or trio has a Bible and a small mirror. Point to the prepared papers on the wall. **What's wrong with the words on these papers? I can't read them! What can you do to find out what the words and numbers say?** Assign each prepared paper to a pair or trio. **Use your mirrors to find out what the words say. When you have read the passage, talk about what it says and think of a good question like the ones we brainstormed earlier on our pictures-and-question papers.**

Pairs or trios decipher words, read the assigned Scripture passage and write on the paper their answers to "What question could you ask to help you 'do what it says'?"

You can write more than one question if you like. If you want to take the challenge, use a mirror to write your questions backwards! If you'd rather write your questions in the normal way, that's also fine.

Conclusion: Many people talk about the importance of reading God's Word, but we've just discovered some good reasons why it's just as important to pay attention to doing what God's Word says. When we're members of God's family, we can depend on God's promise to help us as we follow Him and obey His Word. If you have questions about what it means to be a member of God's family, let me know. I'd like to talk with you. If any team member indicates interest in becoming a member of God's family, arrange a time to talk (see "Leading a Student to Christ" on p. 39).

© 2004 Gospel Light. Permission to photocopy granted. *Raising Up Spiritual Champions*

2. Playbook Preparation

Materials: *Session 3 Student Page* (pp. 93-94) for each team member, What's My Question? posters, pencils, hand mirrors as needed.

Procedure: Distribute *Student Pages* and pencils to team members. Team members fill in answers in "The Write Stuff" section, using hand mirrors if needed. **Be sure to use your mirror to help you! Don't forget to write down both the Bible references and the question for the ones you choose. You will need both during this coming week.**

Check-Off Time: Team members who completed a *Session 2 Student Page* may show their completed

pages to you and recite the Session 2 Bible Memory Verse during this time. As time permits, talk with team members about what they have done. **When is a good time at home for you to work on your *Student Page*? What part of the challenge is hardest for you? Easiest?**

RALLY (10-20 minutes)

Materials: *Champions Music* CD and player, each team member's *Session 3 Student Page*, *Session 3 Parent Page* (pp. 95-96) for each team member, pencils.

Worship: To signal Rally time, play "I Want to Follow Jesus" from *Champions Music* CD. As team members assemble, invite them to sing along with "I Want to Follow Jesus." (Optional: If team members have prepared cheers or raps as suggested on p. 72, invite team members to demonstrate cheers or raps now.)

Share a prayer request or reason to praise God and then invite team members to share prayer requests. **Today, we talked about evaluating our actions by God's Word. Let's listen to this song about obeying God's Word. Listen and let the words of the song help you pray silently. Let's all ask God to help us be disciples of Jesus and put the things we learned into action this week. God doesn't say that He will make us change or force us to follow Him. But day by day as we seek to**

follow Jesus, God will help us grow to be more like Him. Play part or all of "Do What It Says" from *Champions Music* CD. Close in prayer. (Optional: Coaches lead groups of 8 to 12 team members in prayer time. If you started a record of prayer requests during earlier sessions, refer to it during this prayer time.)

Wrap-Up: Point out the activities described on the second side of the *Session 3 Student Page*. Invite any questions about The Challenge. **Each of you chose passages and questions to copy down for The Write Stuff. So "doing what it says" will be different for each of you. But we can all practice putting God's truth into action!**

Be sure every team member leaves with his or her playbook or *Session 3 Student Page* and *Session 3 Parent Page*.

© 2004 Gospel Light. Permission to photocopy granted. *Raising Up Spiritual Champions*

---cut---

Ephesians 4:25-27

Read these verses. Choose one thing the verses say to do.
What question could you ask to help you "do what it says"?
Write the question below.

---cut---

Ephesians 4:29,31

Read these verses. Choose one thing the verses say to do.
What question could you ask to help you "do what it says"?
Write the question below.

---cut---

Ephesians 4:32

Read this verse. Choose one thing the verse says to do.
What question could you ask to help you "do what it says"?
Write the question below.

---cut---

Ephesians 5:4

Read this verse. Choose one thing this verse says to do.
What question could you ask to help you "do what it says"?
Write the question below.

---cut---

Colossians 3:16

Read this verse. Choose one thing this verse says to do.
What question could you ask to help you "do what it says"?
Write the question below.

---cut---

1 Thessalonians 5:15

Read this verse. Choose one thing this verse says to do.
What question could you ask to help you "do what it says"?
Write the question below.

---cut---

1 Thessalonians 5:16-18

Read these verses. Choose one thing these verses say to do.
What question could you ask to help you "do what it says"?
Write the question below.

---cut---

Titus 3:1-2

Read these verses. Choose one thing the verses say to do.
What question could you ask to help you "do what it says"?
Write the question below.

---cut---

© 2004 Gospel Light. Permission to photocopy granted. *Raising Up Spiritual Champions*

The Write Stuff

Look at each completed poster from What's My Question? Then choose three passages and questions to copy into the spaces below. Use a mirror if needed!

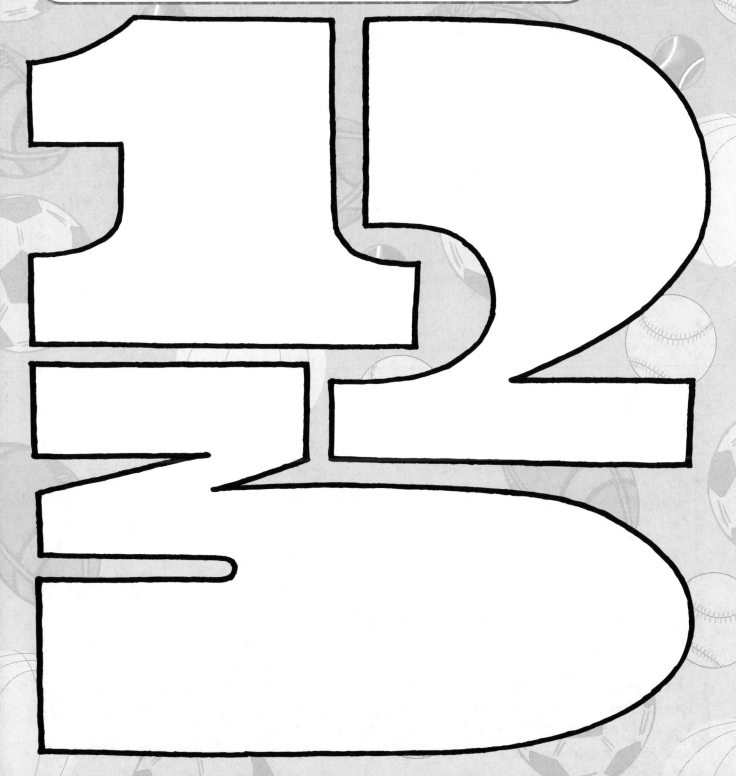

THE CHALLENGE

This session's Bible Memory Verse:

"Show me your ways, O Lord, teach me your paths; guide me in your truth and teach me, for you are God my Savior, and my hope is in you all day long." Psalm 25:4-5

Bible Memory Verse repeated.
Coach's initials

Session 3 page completed.
Coach's initials

Family Challenge

With at least one other family member, stand in front of a mirror. Look carefully. What do you see about yourselves that looks similar? That looks different? Now look at yourselves in a shiny item that is not a mirror such as a car window. What can you see of the similarities and differences you saw in the mirror?

Talk About: What jobs can't be done without a good mirror? The Bible says God's Word is like a mirror. We look into God's Word to know what is true.

Imagination Questions: How would life be different if there were no mirrors at all? How would life be different if the only mirror you had was cracked and dirty? If you could invent a better mirror, what would you change?

Did it!
Parent's initials

The Show Me, Teach Me, Guide Me Method to Put God's Truth into Action!

TRY IT!
On a separate sheet of paper, draw three columns. Write "Show," "Teach" and "Guide" at the top of each column.

SHOW ME
Choose a passage you copied down for The Write Stuff. Look it up and read it. What does this passage show you? If you were going to draw this passage, what would you draw?

TEACH ME
Read the same passage again. Anything here you did not know before? What does this passage **teach** you? If you were going to explain what you've learned to someone else, what would you say?

GUIDE ME
Read the same passage one more time. Now read the question you copied! Is it the same one that you would ask yourself now that you've read this passage three times? Based on this passage, what might God **guide** you to start doing? What might His truth **guide** you to stop doing?

Did it!
Parent's initials

This week, decide to do one of the things you think God is guiding you to do. Write at the bottom of the paper how it went! You don't have to show your paper to anyone. It's for you alone.

Bonus: Do the same thing with the other two passages you copied down in The Write Stuff. You won't get any points, but it will be fun to find out what happens!

© 2004 Gospel Light. Permission to photocopy granted. *Raising Up Spiritual Champions*

How Does Knowing the Truth Make a Difference in My Life?

For more information about this week's question, read James 1:22-27 and James 3:1-3, the sources for our Bible study. You may also read Ephesians 4:25-32 and 1 Thessalonians 5:15-18.

Making Family Devotional Times Count!

In an informal survey of Christian adults, some remember family devotional times as boring, uncomfortable or embarrassing. Others, however, remember devotional times that were engaging, lively and meaningful. Since the goal of our family devotional times should be to focus our hearts on God as a family, we certainly don't want these times to become a duty, a burden or a guilt-producing activity. Rather, times that are joyful, warm and interactive will build relationships within our families as we build a family relationship with God!

While it is through everyday living that we teach our children what we really believe about God and what we really think of living as followers of Jesus, the very act of taking time to think about and worship God together sends powerful messages to our children as well. It reminds us that God sees and loves us as a family as well as individuals. By taking the time to worship God as a family, we show that we think God is important enough to worship at home as well as in a church service.

Here are a few guidelines and ideas for creating positive family devotional times:

First, don't let guilt either burden you or motivate you. ("We don't do this consistently" or "We're not good at this" are feelings commonly expressed.) This is an opportunity to enjoy God and family, not a box to be checked off or a duty to be done! Do what you can, when you can. There is no condemnation to those who are in Christ Jesus!

© 2004 Gospel Light. Permission to photocopy granted. *Raising Up Spiritual Champions*

☺ Bedtime and mealtime provide natural opportunities to turn our hearts to God.

Use one of these times to read one Bible verse, one page from a book of children's devotionals or of questions kids ask about God.

Ask questions, make up rhymes about the subject or play games to keep everyone engaged. You'll be able to tell if these times have meaning for your children by how much they pay attention!

Close the time with a short prayer when children begin to lose interest. And do your best not to create guilt for not listening intently. You'll soon be able to gauge just the right length of time and mix of activities for your family!

☺ Consider special family devotions during the Christmas season. Use an interactive, child-friendly book to guide you. Lighting candles, singing carols and setting up a nativity set can build a family tradition that helps everyone unwind and focus on the meaning of Christmas. (If you're inspired to continue devotional times, you'll already have a grasp of what will work best for your family!)

☺ Consider incorporating a family devotional time into a regular "family time" planned for once a week or once a month.

Second, consider the ages and stages of your children:

If you have a wide range of ages from preschoolers to older children, keep the time brief and everyone involved with a high level of activity. Be sure the older children know they are your helpers in sharing what they know with the younger children!

☺ Try reading a story from a children's Bible. Then invite the younger children to act it out while older children read the story again line by line.

☺ Try assigning a motion to a word that repeats often in the story (e.g., hugging oneself whenever the word "love" is heard).

☺ Try making up motions for a Bible verse, singing a song together that relates to the story or passage or pretending to be a Bible character for children to question.

☺ Especially as children grow older, consider reading a chapter of a book at bedtime that has spiritual implications, such as *The Lion, the Witch and the Wardrobe*. (If you need help to put the spiritual aspects into words, many books are available.) Discussions about the story action of such books and the ideas behind them can form the foundation for talks about important life issues.

Find the formula that works for your family. Keep it simple and lively. You and your children will enjoy great benefit together!

© 2004 Gospel Light. Permission to photocopy granted. *Raising Up Spiritual Champions*

The Coach's Corner

It's easy to grow preoccupied with what the world calls success. Our preoccupation often funnels down to our children as pressure to be straight-A students, superstar athletes, outstanding artists—always to be far above average! Making mediocre grades or being just one of the kids on the team isn't enough. And it's unthinkable that our kids might be failures!

In fact, when we sin and fail to love and obey God, the world teaches us to deny, deny, deny and, when we can't deny any longer, to admit only that unintentional mistakes were made. To admit that I am a sinner or to take personal responsibility for my sin is even more unthinkable than being mediocre.

But the Bible declares we *are* sinners. We *all* fail, fall and sin. Peter, one of Jesus' most confident disciples, failed Jesus in the moments of His greatest need. God's grace loudly declares that we, too—no matter how much we want to think ourselves able, successful and competent—fail to love and obey God. We are completely unable to do anything to make amends with God. Paul called it being "dead in our sins." But the good news is (as one songwriter said, tongue-in-cheek), "Jesus is for losers."

Jesus has never been impressed with those whom the world calls successful. And He has never rejected us because of our sin and our failure to love and obey Him! A broken heart and a contrite spirit are the open door through which His forgiveness enters. Jesus loves losers because they are ready to admit they are sinners and let Him forgive them, love them and fill them with His power so that they are able to do things far beyond what the world's most successful people ever imagined!

BIBLE MEMORY VERSE

"Have mercy on me, O God, according to your unfailing love; according to your great compassion blot out my transgressions. Wash away all my iniquity and cleanse me from my sin." Psalm 51:1-2

Scripture Study

John 13:37-38; 18:15-26; 21:1-19

Aims:

1. To identify effects of failure to love and obey God

2. To discover that God's forgiveness is bigger than our failure to love and obey Him

3. To evaluate our actions, ask God's forgiveness and plan ways to make a fresh start

© 2004 Gospel Light. Permission to photocopy granted. *Raising Up Spiritual Champions*

Session Game Plan

WARM-UP (10-20 minutes)

Materials: *Champions Music* CD and player, Case Study Cards (p. 105), scissors, three large sheets of butcher paper, masking tape, marker, a soft ball.

Procedure: Play a game, passing a ball behind their backs, and then talk about and chart effects of failure to love and obey God.

POWER-UP (20-30 minutes)

Materials: Bible for each team member, Peter's Interview Cards (pp. 107-108), scissors, envelope.

Procedure: Use Peter's Interview Cards to interview an adult who pretends to be Peter and answers questions about sin, failure and forgiveness.

PRACTICE (20-30 minutes)

Materials: *Session 4 Student Page* (pp. 109-110) for each team member, The Rest of the Story Cards (p. 106), scissors, an inflated balloon for each group of four to five team members, brainstorming posters from Warm-Up, masking tape, pencils.

Procedure: Team members play a relay game to collect The Rest of the Story Cards and then use cards to complete the third category of brainstorming posters begun in Warm-Up. Team members discuss and apply the information to complete The Write Stuff in the *Session 4 Student Page*.

RALLY (10-20 minutes)

Materials: *Champions Music* CD and player, each team member's *Session 4 Student Page*, *Session 4 Parent Page* (pp. 111-112) for each team member, pencils.

Procedure: Sing worship songs, talk about the week's assignment and pray together.

© 2004 Gospel Light. Permission to photocopy granted. *Raising Up Spiritual Champions*

WARM-UP (10-20 minutes)

The Ripple Effect

Materials: *Champions Music* CD and player, Case Study Cards (p. 105), scissors, three large sheets of butcher paper, masking tape, marker, a soft ball.

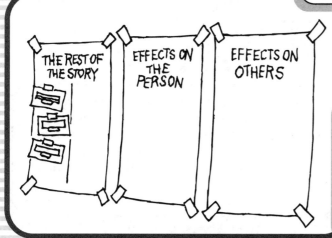

Preparation: Photocopy and cut apart a set of Case Study Cards. Tape sheets of butcher paper to wall and write each of the following categories at the top of each separate paper: "Effects on the Person," "Effects on Others" and "The Rest of the Story" (see sketch). Draw a vertical line to make two columns on "The Rest of the Story" poster.

Procedure: Team members stand in a circle. Give one team member the ball. **We're going to play a game like Hot Potato with this ball—except you have to pass the ball behind your backs. Pass the ball behind your back around the circle while the music plays. When the music stops, the person holding the ball may read one of these cards aloud or give it to another person to read.** Play "I Want to Follow Jesus" from *Champions Music* CD as ball is passed around the circle. After 10-15 seconds, stop music. Team member holding ball reads card or gives card to another to read and then tapes card to left column of The Rest of the Story poster (see sketch). Repeat until all cards are read aloud and taped to the poster.

Then ask the questions below, writing responses in appropriate categories on the appropriate posters. Continue until all cards are read and discussed. (Note: Posters will be used later in the session.)

🖋 **How did this person's actions affect him or her?** (Write answers on "Effects on the Person" poster.)

🖋 **What feelings do you think this situation caused for this person? What else might this person have thought about the situation?** (Write answers on "Effects on the Person" poster.)

🖋 **What do you think might have been the effects of this situation on the person's family members?** (Write answers on "Effects on Others" poster.)

🖋 **What do you think might have been the effects on this person's friends, classmates or others?** (Write answers on "Effects on Others" poster.)

Conclusion: How are all of these stories the same? (They focus on failure to love and obey God.) We all fail, sin and do wrong sometimes. Point to the brainstorming poster lettered, "The Rest of the Story." But the stories we've read don't end here. Later, we'll complete this poster and find out the rest of these stories!

© 2004 Gospel Light. Permission to photocopy granted. *Raising Up Spiritual Champions*

POWER-UP (20-30 minutes)

Materials: Bible for each team member, Peter's Interview Cards (pp. 107-108), scissors, envelope.

LIVE OPTION!

Increase interest and interaction by inviting a guest to dress in a Bible-times costume and be prepared to respond to the interview questions as Peter.

Preparation: Photocopy and cut apart two sets of Peter's Interview Cards. Store one set in an envelope for use during class. Give the other set to the person who will be answering as Peter so that he or she can prepare answers, looking up Scripture verses noted on cards.

Procedure: Distribute the interview cards to volunteers. Be sure each team member has a Bible. **We've already heard about three people whose stories seem to be ending in sin and failure. We know we sin and fail, too.**

Let's pretend to be in Bible times to interview one of Jesus' best-known disciples. We're going to find out what he says about a time he failed to love and obey God. This disciple really blew it! Give other hints about Peter's life as needed. **Which disciple do you think it was?**

You (or another adult) play the role of Peter. **Interviewers, ask Peter the questions on your cards in numbered order. Our goal is to find out what happened to Peter and what happens to us when we sin and fail to love and obey God.**

Students ask the questions, one at a time, in numbered order. The person playing the role of Peter answers the questions telling about Peter's life as a disciple, about his denial of Jesus, about how Jesus forgave him and about how God later used Peter. Encourage team members who are not asking the questions to find the passages noted on the cards.

2

In the same conversation, you also declared that you had come to believe and know that Jesus is the One whom God promised to send and that He is God's Son. Tell us how you felt when you made those statements.

© 2004 Gospel Light. Permission to photocopy granted. *Raising Up Spiritual Champions*

Peter loved Jesus. He believed in Jesus. He thought he loved Jesus enough to die for him. But when Peter thought he was in danger, he lied and denied he even knew Jesus! He sinned, and he failed his dearest friend.

Jesus could have said, "Well, Peter denied he even knows Me. I'll just forget about him!" But Jesus did not give up on Peter. He forgave Peter. Jesus loved Peter and let Peter know that he had a great future. Later, Peter went on to do even greater things than the ones about which we read!

☺ **What are ways that kids your age fail to obey God?** (Cheat in a game. Get in trouble at school. Lie. Hurt someone.) **The Bible calls these actions "sin." Sin is doing things our own way instead of doing things God's way. Sin is failing to love and obey God.**

☺ **Are there any sins that are unforgivable by God? Why or why not? When we fail to love and obey God, what does God think** about us? **What does the Bible say about sin?** Ask a volunteer to read 1 John 1:9 aloud.

☺ **What does this verse say we have to do to be forgiven?**

☺ **What do you think the word "confess" means?** (Admit our sin to God. Tell Him we want to love and obey Him in the future and ask for His help.)

Conclusion: Peter learned that God's forgiveness is bigger than all his failures. Jesus doesn't give up on any of us, either. His Word says that if we confess our sins, He will forgive us and help us obey. God's forgiveness is bigger than our sin! And God's forgiveness is what makes it possible for us to be members of God's family and be His disciples. If any team member indicates interest in becoming a member of God's family, arrange a time to talk (see "Leading a Student to Christ" on p. 39).

For more references to Peter's later life, invite team members to pair up and find one or more of the following references: Acts 3:1-9; 10; 12:1-19. Invite each pair to tell one thing they learned about Peter's later life through the passage they read.

© 2004 Gospel Light. Permission to photocopy granted. *Raising Up Spiritual Champions*

PRACTICE (20-30 minutes)

1. Balloon Relay!

Materials: The Rest of the Story Cards (p. 106), scissors, an inflated balloon for each group of four to five team members.

Preparation: Photocopy and cut apart one set of The Rest of the Story cards.

Procedure: Teams of four to five team members each play a relay game. Teams line up on one side of the classroom. Give the first team member in each line an inflated balloon. At your signal, the first team member in each line taps the balloon up into the air as he or she moves to the other side of the playing area and back. The second team member in line then taps the balloon across the playing area and back while holding the wrist of the first team member (see sketch). Game continues until the whole team is holding wrists and moving across the playing area and back as the last team member taps the balloon. Award a card to the team that wins the relay. Play until all cards have been awarded.

GAME EXPANSION!

1. To increase the action, play a relay game outdoors. Team members take turns kicking a playground ball across a large play area into a large cardboard box.

2. For an alternate game, have a treasure hunt by hiding The Rest of the Story Cards indoors or outdoors.

© 2004 Gospel Light. Permission to photocopy granted. *Raising Up Spiritual Champions*

2. The Rest of the Story

Materials: Brainstorming posters from Warm-Up, The Rest of the Story Cards used in the previous activity, masking tape.

Preparation: Invite team members to gather near the brainstorming posters. Team members holding The Rest of the Story Cards take turns to read cards aloud. Team members then consult in order to match cards to the correct situations. Team member holding card tapes it in the right column on The Rest of the Story poster to complete the appropriate story.

After cards are matched, ask:

🖋 **Which story do you think had the most surprising ending? Why?**

🖋 **Whose story was the least surprising? Why?**

🖋 **What things might have happened between the beginnings and the endings of these stories?**

🖋 **Describe ways God gave each of these people a fresh start.**

🖋 **What do you think these people would say about God's forgiveness and help to make a fresh start?**

🖋 **What would you tell a kid your age who has failed by disobeying God? What would you want that person to know about making a fresh start?**

3. Playbook Preparation

Materials: *Session 4 Student Page* (pp. 109-110) for each team member, pencils.

Procedure: Distribute *Student Pages* and pencils. Invite teammates to fill out "The Write Stuff" portions of their pages. **We're going to pretend to be writers of an advice column. To finish these sentences with some good advice, think about the people whose lives we have studied today and remember the words of 1 John 1:9.**

Check-Off Time: Team members who completed *Session 3 Student Pages* may show their completed pages to you and recite the previous week's Bible Memory Verse during this time. As time permits, ask questions about their at-home assignments. **What did you especially enjoy about your challenge this week? With whom did you do your Family Challenge?**

RALLY (10-20 minutes)

Materials: *Champions Music* CD and player, each team member's *Session 4 Student* Page, *Session 4 Parent Page* (pp. 111-112) for each team member, pencils

Worship: Take time to listen to "Psalm 51:1-4,10-12" from *Champions Music* CD. **This song reminds us that God loves us and will forgive us when we sin. He will help us make a fresh start when we ask His help!** Sing "I Want to Follow Jesus" together.

Ask about answers to last week's prayer requests. Share a reason to praise God or a prayer request and then invite team members to share requests. **During our silent prayer time, let's think about times we have failed to obey God and reasons we need forgiveness.** Have a short time of silent prayer.

Thank You, God, for Your love. Thank You for Your promise to forgive our sins when we confess them to You. Please help us to plan ways to make a fresh start. In Jesus' name, amen. (Optional: Coaches lead groups of 8 to 12 team members in prayer time. If you started a record of prayer requests during earlier sessions, refer to it during this prayer time.)

Wrap-Up: Look at side two of the *Student Page* with team members. Invite questions about any of the assignments. Be sure every team member leaves with his or her *Session 4 Student Page* and a *Session 4 Parent Page*.

© 2004 Gospel Light. Permission to photocopy granted. *Raising Up Spiritual Champions*

Case Study Cards

1 I've been stealing money from my father for years. I don't think he believes the lies I tell to cover up, but he's only REALLY caught me once. Not long ago, he sent me away to school—to become a minister! What a joke! Now I steal from the school—and from my teachers and friends. I sneak out of hotels and restaurants without paying. Even when I went to prison, it didn't stop me: I'm still stealing—and lying about it. I'm a total failure at being honest!

2 I've played the piano since I was 3! I started writing songs when I was young, too. I wrote and recorded a song when I was only 12! People were telling me I would be the next big star. I was going to be rich and famous! But another kid became the big star instead. I didn't get the fame, the recording deals or the money. I feel like I was cheated out of my future. I ran away from home. Now I've tried lots of drugs and hurt lots of people—all the kinds of things a failure does.

3 I'm just a poor kid. Most of my brothers and sisters died as little children. My father is an alcoholic. He lost his job, so we had to move. He treated my mother and me very badly. We had no money for food. So by the time I was 10, I worked hard for half a day and went to school half a day. I grew angry at my life. What future could there be for a poor girl with a drunken father? So I started to hang out with the street gangs in my town. I'm wild and mean and I don't care! My life is destined for failure.

© 2004 Gospel Light. Permission to photocopy granted. *Raising Up Spiritual Champions*

The Rest of the Story Cards

A friend told me about a prayer meeting nearby. Since I was studying to be a minister, he thought I should go. Wow! The people at this meeting were full of love and joy! I realized I needed a fresh start. I asked God to forgive my sin. I gave my whole life to Jesus Christ—and He did give me a fresh start! He helped me stop lying! He helped me never want to steal again!

Later, I opened many homes and schools to give orphans and poor children a fresh start, too. I opened a school to teach people about the Bible and spent years going around the world to tell the good news of Jesus. Since God gave me, a lying thief, a fresh start, I have never asked a person for money. My Father in heaven has taken care of me every day!

Who am I?

George Müller, founder of orphanages, teacher, missionary, pastor—and former thief.

I met a beautiful girl named Melody. Her life had been sad, too! But we loved each other and we got married. And then I met Jesus Christ! He forgave my sins and gave me a fresh start! He took away my anger. I began to write new songs that told how glad I was that Jesus had come into my life! Soon, I sang and played those songs everywhere. We gave concerts, made recordings, opened our home to other hurting people. God gave me a new start, new life and new songs!

Who am I?

Keith Green, musician, evangelist—and former failure in life and in the music business.

There was an old lady in my neighborhood. She was kind to me and told me about Jesus. I gave my life to Jesus and that changed everything! I started teaching Bible classes for the children in my town. Then I heard about the sad things that were going on in a part of Africa. I decided to go there and see what I could do to help! I learned the language and lived in Africa for the rest of my life. Over the years, I saved the lives of many babies, women and children and taught people about Jesus.

Who am I?

Mary Slessor—missionary, teacher—and former child who didn't seem to have a future.

© 2004 Gospel Light. Permission to photocopy granted. *Raising Up Spiritual Champions*

Peter's Interview Cards

1

Peter, when Jesus asked you if you wanted to stop following Him, you said no. In John 6:68, what reason did you give him?

2

In the same conversation, you also declared that you had come to believe and know that Jesus is the One whom God promised to send and that He is God's Son. Tell us how you felt when you made those statements.

3

In John 13:37, you stated your commitment to Jesus. What did you tell Jesus you would do?

4

You said in John 13:38 that you were prepared to die for Jesus. What did Jesus say to you? How did you feel when Jesus responded as He did? Why did you think He said this?

5

Not long after this, you were reported to be with Jesus in the Garden of Gethsemane. In John 18:1-11, we read that you tried to protect Jesus when soldiers came to arrest Him. What did you do? How did Jesus feel about what you did?

6

We're curious about what happened at the high priest's house. We understand from John 18:15-17 that John went inside but you were stopped at the door. What happened?

© 2004 Gospel Light. Permission to photocopy granted. *Raising Up Spiritual Champions*

According to John 18:18,25, you had another chance to tell people that Jesus was your friend. What did you do?

It's reported in John 18:26-27 that yet another servant, a relative of the very man whose ear you had cut off, recognized you! He asked, "Didn't I see you with Him?" What did you say? What happened then? How did you feel?

When you first heard that Jesus was dead, how did you feel? In Mark 16:6-7 it says that when Jesus rose, the angel told the women to tell you specifically that He would meet you in Galilee. How did you feel then? What did you see in the empty tomb? How did it make you feel?

We understand from reading John 21:1-19 that Jesus met you by the lake in Galilee. After your breakfast with Him, He asked you some specific questions. What did Jesus ask? What did you answer? What do you think Jesus meant for you to do? What would you say about Jesus' forgiveness?

After God sent the Holy Spirit, we read in Acts 2:37-42 that there was quite a change in you! Tell us what happened that day.

© 2004 Gospel Light. Permission to photocopy granted. *Raising Up Spiritual Champions*

What Happens When I Sin?

The Write Stuff

Someone needs your help and advice! Finish each sentence starter. Don't forget to look at the Bible Memory Verse on the other side of this page and 1 John 1:9 for ideas, too!

Dear Advice Person,

When my dad asked if I had studied for a math test at school, I lied. I said I had studied. But I failed the test! Now my dad will find out I lied. What can I do? Is there any hope for me?

Signed,

Dopey

Dear Dopey,

I'm glad to tell you that . . .

God says . . .

You can . . .

Sincerely,

Dear Giver of Advice,

I've done something really bad. No one else knows—yet. What should I do?

Signed,

Feeling Rotten

Dear Feeling Rotten,

You don't have to . . .

The Bible says . . .

I'd suggest that you . . .

Sincerely,

© 2004 Gospel Light. Permission to photocopy granted. *Raising Up Spiritual Champions*

THE CHALLENGE

This session's Bible Memory Verse:

"Have mercy on me, O God, according to your unfailing love; according to your great compassion blot out my transgressions. Wash away all my iniquity and cleanse me from my sin." Psalm 51:1-2

Bible Memory Verse repeated.
Coach's initials

Session 4 page completed.
Coach's initials

Using a marker or crayon, draw on a sheet of paper a doodle that looks like a mistake. Then add some lines to create a picture from the mistake. How is what happened to this mistake like something in your life? Think of a way you have learned from a sinful mistake to serve God better.

Did it!
Parent's initials

On another sheet of paper, write down two things you can do this week that will help you make a fresh start with God's help. Put that paper where you will see it every day. Check at the end of the week to see how you did!

Did it!
Parent's initials

Family Challenge

Using an audiocassette recorder, video camera or other recording device, record a story about how God has turned failure and sin into a fresh start! Ask an older friend or family member, "What can you tell me about a time you failed to obey God and God forgave you and helped you?" With the person's permission, show or play your finished recording to a friend or to family members.

Talk About: What does God's Word say about forgiveness? (See 1 John 1:9.) What does it say about forgiving others? (See Matthew 6:14-15.) What can you do to promote forgiveness at home?

Imagination Questions: What do you think would happen if no one in our house forgave anyone for a day? For a week? How do you think (Jon) would feel? How do you think (Mom) would act? Thank God together for forgiveness and fresh starts!

Did it!
Parent's initials

Family Challenge Bonus

Try this experiment! Place one cup water in a clear glass and add three drops of blue food coloring. Add one-half cup of bleach. Stir and let stand. What happens to the water? What do you learn from this experiment about what happens when God forgives our sin?

Did it!
Parent's initials

© 2004 Gospel Light. Permission to photocopy granted. *Raising Up Spiritual Champions*

For more information about this week's question, read John 13:37-38, 18:15-26, 21:1-19, the sources for our Bible study. You may also read Acts 3:1-9; 10; 12:1-19.

Never Picked Last!

Some of us grew up with both natural athletic ability and the gift of adults who trained us in the finer points of a sport. We were often team captains, centers, pitchers, quarterbacks and goalies. Our bodies became finely tuned machines that did our bidding, winning us games, praise and the acceptance of everyone.

Then there are those of us who grew up uncoordinated and lumpy. Our bodies failed us at critical moments: We tripped over the kickball when it came barreling to the plate. We thought we had thrown a perfect free throw only to watch it fly wide off the backboard.

Every time we threw hard from left field, our throws never quite made it to the play where it was needed. Consequently, long before elementary school was over, we knew—as did everyone else—that we were at the bottom of the sports pecking order, the untouchables of the playground.

The consequence was that we were always picked last for whatever team was formed. The pain of our failure became so great that eventually we did our best to stay away from any sports activity that would humiliate us.

None of this has changed. The rejection and pain of being picked last, of being uncoordinated or of being a detriment to your team continues on in every school, every day. But the good news is this: Jesus has never picked you last for His team.

Rather, He says, "I picked you before you were born! I made you. I know you and I love you. In fact, I'm going to help you to become

© 2004 Gospel Light. Permission to photocopy granted. *Raising Up Spiritual Champions*

more than you hoped and dreamed you could be, in spite of your failure and sin. I'm on your side and I'm staying right here all the way!" That's a VERY different kind of team than what we are used to being part of—whether we're adults or children. But that is exactly the kind of team for which Jesus chooses us!

Because we use the paradigm and language of sports in **Raising Up Spiritual Champions,** it's important to reeducate your children to this new team. Tell your children over and over that on Jesus' team, everyone matters.

Nobody blows it so badly that they are kicked off the team.

Your actions of acceptance and grace to your child will be a far more powerful means of educating them in the finer points of discipleship than any words you could ever say. Help your child see that in Jesus' view, we're just touchdowns waiting to happen, goals waiting to be made, perfect free throws about to swish through the net! That is what living in and trusting His grace is all about.

© 2004 Gospel Light. Permission to photocopy granted. *Raising Up Spiritual Champions*

Where Do I Go For Answers?

5
Session

The Coach's Corner

It has been said that the only yardstick for success is being a champion. The popular icon of a successful champion is a tough and independent-minded soul who is always first, who trusts no one and never asks for anything (not even directions when lost!). This attitude is so often modeled in literature, TV shows, movies and video games that it can begin to feel normal to Christians. But what kind of champion follows Jesus? What is God's yardstick for success?

Caleb and Joshua were just such champions in God's eyes. Their actions help us remember that trusting and obeying God is the basis for a life that wins (as opposed to the view that only winning makes a life!). They were the voices of faith in a loud chorus of self-focused doubt and woe from those who had returned from surveying the land! Caleb and Joshua may have been as terrified by the giants as the rest of the spies were—but their focus was on God. They chose to believe what God had said. They chose to trust that obeying His plan would empower them to take over the land, giants notwithstanding! God honored their faith and, years later, gave them the privilege of leading a new, believing generation into His Promised Land.

Even the most independent winner draws every breath and heartbeat from a God whose love is far beyond imagination. We are all *totally* dependent on God's grace! When we acknowledge our dependence on God and ask Him to help us show our trust by our obedient actions, we're on the fast track to being champions in His eyes! The world's model of success may be insistently presented, but it need not be our model. Jesus is! He trusted God fully and obeyed God completely. God is ready to make long-term winners out of those who look to Him, trust Him and obey their way to victory through His power!

BIBLE MEMORY VERSE

"Stand firm. Let nothing move you. Always give yourself fully to the work of the Lord."
1 Corinthians 15:58

Scripture Study

Numbers 13:1-2, 17-33; 14:1-10

Aims:

1. To discuss how Caleb and Joshua trusted God and showed their faith

2. To discover that when we trust in God's Word and obey it, God makes us able to stand firm in our faith

3. To plan ways to make trusting God's Word part of our lives every day

© 2004 Gospel Light. Permission to photocopy granted. *Raising Up Spiritual Champions*

Session Game Plan

WARM-UP (10-20 minutes)

Materials: Rope, 3-6 feet (.9-1.8 m) long; masking tape; three large sheets of butcher paper; marker; four large plastic garbage bags for every six to eight team members.

Procedure: Play a tug-of-war game and then talk about what it means to stand firm and times when it is difficult to stand firm in what you believe.

POWER-UP (20-30 minutes)

Materials: Bible for each team member, "Mission: Possible?" (pp. 121-123), What Happened Next? Cards (p. 124), scissors, spy costumes and props.

Procedure: Read or act out a skit and then study Bible passages to discuss ways Caleb and Joshua showed they trusted God.

PRACTICE (20-30 minutes)

Materials: Bible and *Session 5 Student Page* (pp. 129-130) for each team member, Distraction! Cards and Verse Cards (pp. 125-126), scissors, obstacle-course items (broom, chair, table, hula hoop, yarn), Challenges and Bible Verse posters from Warm-Up, masking tape, marker, pencils.

Procedure: Team members play an obstacle course game to gather Bible Verse cards and add Bible verses and ideas to the poster from Warm-Up. Each student then completes The Write Stuff on his or her *Session 5 Student Page*.

RALLY (10-20 minutes)

Materials: *Champions Music* CD and player, each team member's *Session 5 Student Page*, Amazing Itty-Bitty Bible Journal (pp. 127-128) and *Session 5 Parent Page* (pp. 131-132) for each team member, pencils.

Procedure: Sing worship songs, talk about the week's assignment and pray together.

© 2004 Gospel Light. Permission to photocopy granted. *Raising Up Spiritual Champions*

WARM-UP (10-20 minutes)

Standing Firm

Materials: Rope, 3-6 feet (.9-1.8 m) long; masking tape; three large sheets of butcher paper; marker; four large plastic garbage bags for every six to eight team members.

Preparation: Arrange for a large, open area in which to play this game. Make a masking-tape line in the center of the game area. Write "Strategies" at the top of one sheet of paper. Write "Challenges" at the top of the second sheet. Write "Bible Verses" at top of the third sheet. Tape all three sheets to the wall, taping Challenges and Bible Verse posters next to each other. (Note: Posters will be used later in the session.)

Provide a variety of ways for team members to experiment with their ability to stand firm. If you have access to an outdoor area, team members can experiment with firm footing by trying the challenge first on grass (with or without shoes) or in sand. Indoors, they may try the challenge with or without shoes on carpet.

To help team members think of additional times it's hard to stand firm in their faith, ask, **What are times you might feel confused? Afraid? Not sure of what to do?** Give several age-appropriate examples from your own life.

Procedure: Divide into even-numbered groups of no more than six to eight team members each. **What helps a team to win at tug-of-war?** (Weight. Position. Firm footing.) **It's very important to have firm footing. Today we face the Standing Firm challenge! We're going to play several rounds of tug-of-war but with a challenge. During the first round, we'll play while standing on slippery plastic bags. Then you can try different things or experiment with different strategies to help you stand firm.** Each group divides in half, takes a rope and plays a round of tug-of-war standing on plastic bags or in a way listed in Slam Dunk. The team that pulls first member of opposing team over the line wins.

After first round, use the marker to take notes on the poster titled "Strategies" as team members answer the following questions:

🖊 **Describe how it feels to lose your footing. What happened next?**

🖊 **What did you try to improve your footing? How well did that work?**

Repeat tug-of-war activity as time permits. Invite team members to change strategy with each round to see what helps them stand firm. After each round, ask questions such as:

© 2004 Gospel Light. Permission to photocopy granted. *Raising Up Spiritual Champions*

◖ **What improvements or changes did you make this time? Which strategies worked best?**

◖ **What difference did it make when you (placed a big guy on the end or wrapped the rope around a tree)?**

◖ **Who gave your team the best advice? What was it? What happened?**

◖ **What advice did you take that didn't work so well?**

It's really hard to win this game when you don't have firm footing! Our Bible verse for today, 1 Corinthians 15:58, says, "Stand firm. Let nothing move you. Always give yourself fully to the work of the Lord."

◖ **What do you think this verse means by "stand firm"?** (Keep on believing what you know to be true about God. Keep on trusting God.)

◖ **When you were standing (on the plastic bags), how firm was your footing?**

As the team members answer the following questions, write their answers on the poster titled "Challenges."

◖ **We had some challenges with standing firm while we played our game. But what are some** real-life challenges kids might face at school? At home? (Arguments with brothers and sisters. Getting good grades. Moving to a new school.)

◖ **What are times when it's hard to stand firm in our faith or to trust God?** (When I am afraid. When friends pressure me to do wrong. When I am tempted to lie. When I'm confused. When I find that someone has broken my trust. When I learn that others are not perfect or are hypocrites. When I'm a hypocrite. When family members fight. When someone I love is very sick.)

Conclusion: To win at today's challenge, we had to find ways to stand firm on a slippery surface. Was that easy or hard to do? When things happen to us that confuse us or make us unsure of what to do, we can feel like we are standing on those plastic bags. We don't have firm footing. Our faith in God can feel shaky, as if it's sliding out from under us!

Today we'll meet a couple of spies who were winners in God's eyes because they stood firm when everyone else was confused and shaky. They found that God helps us do what is right when we obey Him.

Costumes and props:

The skit used in the activity on the next page can be done without costumes, props or music, but the humor will increase when cast members wear costumes (trench coats, hats, dark glasses) and carry props (cell phones, walkie-talkies or other high-tech spy gizmos). For more fun, play "spy" music (such as "Theme from Mission: Impossible") and create a bunch of enormous grapes by tying inflated purple balloons together and draping the bunch over a stick for easy carrying be-tween two spies.

© 2004 Gospel Light. Permission to photocopy granted. *Raising Up Spiritual Champions*

POWER-UP (20-30 minutes)

Materials: Bible for each team member, "Mission: Possible?" (pp. 121-123), What Happened Next? Cards (p. 124), scissors, spy costumes and props.

Preparation: Make 6 to 10 copies of "Mission: Possible?" for team members reading the parts of Moses, Joshua, Caleb and 3 to 10 spies. (If desired, hand out scripts ahead of time for team members to study and highlight.) Photocopy and cut apart the What Happened Next? Cards.

Procedure: Volunteers read skit aloud. After the skit is completed, ask:

☺ **What were some of the good things about the land?**

☺ **Why were the spies afraid to take over the land?**

☺ **Who believed they could take the land?**

Divide group into five teams. Distribute one What Happened Next? Card to each group. **Let's get our Bibles. Help each other find the verses you see on your What Happened Next? Card. Let's discover what happened next with Moses, the spies Caleb and Joshua, the Israelite people and God.** Allow time for team members to find and read Bible verses. Volunteers from each team give a summary of or read aloud the verses on their cards.

☺ **What did Caleb and Joshua do that showed they trusted God?**

☺ **What words did Caleb and Joshua say that showed their trust in God?**

☺ **What did God say about Caleb? About Joshua?**

☺ **Who went with Caleb and Joshua to the Promised Land?**

☺ **Who didn't go to the Promised Land? Why?**

☺ **How do you feel when someone calls you a liar? Why?**

Conclusion: The 10 spies and the others who were afraid wanted to go back to Egypt. They were showing by their words that they did not believe God was telling them the truth! Imagine telling God that you think He is a liar!

But Caleb and Joshua believed that God was telling the truth. Because they trusted God, they showed their faith in God. They chose to obey what God had said to do and they encouraged the others to obey God, too. It took 40 years, but the day came when Joshua and Caleb led all the Israelites into the Promised Land. God took care of them, just as He had promised 40 years before! As members of God's family, we can depend on God's promises. If you'd like to know more about being a member of God's family, please let me know. If any team member indicates interest in becoming a member of God's family, arrange a time to talk (see "Leading a Student to Christ" on p. 39).

© 2004 Gospel Light. Permission to photocopy granted. *Raising Up Spiritual Champions*

PRACTICE (20-30 minutes)

1. Distraction! Obstacle Course

Materials: Distraction! Cards and Verse Cards (pp. 125-126), scissors, obstacle-course items (broom, chair, table, hula hoop, yarn), tape.

Preparation: Photocopy and cut apart one set of Distraction! Cards and Verse Cards. Set up an obstacle course (see sketch) in a fairly large playing area. Tape a Distraction! Card to each obstacle item. If possible, station an adult at each obstacle. Place Verse Cards in a stack at the end of the obstacle course.

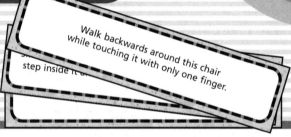

Walk backwards around this chair while touching it with only one finger.

step inside it a...

Procedure: Let's play a game that helps us think about what happens when we're distracted from living as one of Jesus' disciples. Briefly review (and invite a volunteer to demonstrate) the action for each obstacle as outlined on the Distraction! Card. **Our challenge here is to see how quickly each of us can move through our obstacle course. But beware! People may try to distract you or slow you down. You'll need to practice ignoring the distractions. Stay focused to keep moving!** Team members enter the obstacle course at timed intervals to avoid crowding and move through course doing actions described on Distraction! Cards. Adults make sure team members do actions but also may try to distract or slow down team members by talking, asking irrelevant questions, pointing, etc.

(Do not physically restrain players.) As each team member exits the course, he or she takes a Verse Card from the stack. (If the group is larger than number of cards, distribute a card to a pair or trio.)

When team members have completed the course and have collected Verse Cards, ask:

🖋 **How did you feel when you were reading the Distraction! Card and someone was trying to distract you?**

🖋 **Was it easy or hard to trust what the card said to do when people were distracting you?**

🖋 **What strategies did you try to help yourself focus and ignore the distractions? How well did your strategies work?**

© 2004 Gospel Light. Permission to photocopy granted. *Raising Up Spiritual Champions*

2. Plan to Stand

Materials: A Bible for each team member, Verse Cards collected at end of Distraction! Obstacle Course, Challenges and Bible Verse posters from Warm-Up, masking tape, marker.

Procedure: Now we're going to discover some truths in God's Word that can help us stand firm in our faith. These truths can help us stay focused as we move through life so that we won't be distracted from following God and living as a disciple of Jesus. Team members (or pairs or trios) use their Bibles to look up verses listed on Verse Cards they received.

When verses have been found, read aloud the first challenge listed on the Challenges poster from Warm-Up. Ask, **If you think the Bible verse on your card might help a person in this situation, wave your verse card in the air.**

Volunteer reads aloud or paraphrases verse and then tells why he or she thinks the verse might help a person in that situation. If the group agrees, volunteer tapes verse card onto the Bible Verse poster beside the description on the Challenges poster. Write additional comments on the Bible Verse poster as well.

Continue by discussing each challenge described, voting and adding a verse card and appropriate comments beside each challenge. (If there are

fewer cards than situations, write appropriate Bible references beside other situations.)

🔹 If team members have a hard time deciding which verse would best help in a situation, ask:

🔹 **When has something like this happened to you? Why would knowing this verse have helped you?**

🔹 **What advice would you give a person in this situation?**

🔹 **Is there another situation listed in which this verse might be more helpful?**

Conclusion: When we know God's Word, it is like having a firm place to stand. We can go to God's Word for answers when things are confusing and we need to know what is right. When we obey what we know, God helps us to stand firm in our faith!

Alternative Challenge:

Instead of setting up an obstacle course, simply hide Verse Cards and invite team members to find them.

---

3. Playbook Preparation

Materials: Bible and *Session 5 Student Page* (pp. 129-130) for each team member, pencils.

Procedure: Distribute *Student Pages* and pencils to team members. Each team member completes "The Write Stuff" section of his or her *Student Page,* using the Bible as needed to review the verses listed on the Bible Verse poster.

Check-Off Time: Team members who completed *Session 4 Student Pages* may show their completed pages to you and recite the previous week's Bible Memory Verse during this time. Team members may check in at any time during Playbook Preparation

time so that no one has to wait in line. As time permits, talk with team members about their at-home assignments. **What was your favorite part about this week's challenge? How would you say the Bible Memory Verse in your own words?**

RALLY (10-20 minutes)

Materials: *Champions Music* CD and player, each team member's *Session 5 Student Page*, Amazing Itty-Bitty Spiritual Exercise Journal (pp. 127-128) and *Session 5 Parent Page* (pp. 131-132) for each team member, pencils.

Worship: Take time to sing "Trust in the Lord" and/or "I Want to Follow Jesus" from *Champions Music* CD. If time permits, encourage team members to create or practice motions for the song(s) and repeat song(s) several times.

Ask about answers to last week's prayer requests. Share a reason to praise God or a prayer request and then invite team members to share their requests. Team members may write prayer requests in the margins of their *Student Pages*. (Optional: Coaches lead groups of 8 to 12 team members each in prayer time. If you started a record of prayer requests during earlier sessions, refer to it during this prayer time.)

Invite team members to look at side two of their *Student Pages* and then distribute copies of the Amazing Itty-Bitty Spiritual Exercise Journal. Demonstrate how to fold the paper into a weekly journal. **Often, when people are going to try to change the way they eat and exercise, they use journals to write down what they eat and what kind of exercises they do. It helps them think about the ways they want to change. We each have a spiritual exercise journal! It's a way to help us think about the ways we want to grow and change on the inside!**

Your journal doesn't need a lot of writing. But a little writing each day will help you think about what you read. When you read and think about God's Word, you understand more about who God is and how to obey Him. When we obey Him, it helps us to stand firm when things get confusing!

We're going to try some new things this week to help us be disciples of Jesus and learn to stand firm. It's important that we take time to ask God for His help. Take time for silent prayer, or invite volunteers to pray sentence prayers aloud.

Conclude, **Thank You, God, that Your Word tells us what we need to know about standing firm and trusting You. Please help each of us as we try this week to trust Your Word, obey You and learn to stand firm when things get confusing. Help us each day to read and think about Your Word. In Jesus' name, amen.**

Wrap-Up: Look at both sides of the *Student Page* with team members. Be sure they understand the activities on side two. Invite questions about any of the assignments. Be sure every team member leaves with his or her *Student Page*, Amazing Itty-Bitty Spiritual Exercise Journal and *Parent Page*.

© 2004 Gospel Light. Permission to photocopy granted. *Raising Up Spiritual Champions*

Mission: Possible?

Based on Numbers 13:1-2,17-33

CHARACTERS:

MOSES, leader of the Israelites and chief spy guy

JOSHUA, Moses' very military assistant, a brave, bold man sent to spy

CALEB, friend of Joshua and another brave, bold man sent to spy

SPIES (at least 3 and up to 10), brave, bold . . . well, maybe not . . . men sent to spy

SCENE 1:

SPY MUSIC plays. Spies, Joshua and Caleb enter from different areas, dressed as spies, wearing sunglasses and talking on phones, looking around, trying to hide as they enter. They gather around Moses.

MOSES

(Counting on fingers as he speaks.) Well, men, I hope you're all here. It wasn't easy to get the message out. SOME of you have lost your SPY PHONES!

SPIES

(In whiny-voiced unison.) SORRY, sir!

JOSHUA

(Saluting.) Sir, communications still proved effective. We are all present and accounted for, SIR!

SPIES

(In whiny-voiced unison.) We hope this mission doesn't prove IMPOSSIBLE!

MOSES

(Pointing to heaven.) Our missions are NEVER impossible. Here's the plan *(Pretending to unroll a large roll of paper or a map.)*: Move north from here to here. Your mission—and you DO choose to accept it—is to check out the land to see what's there. We need topographic, hydrologic, geologic and anthropologic surveys. I want soil samples, produce samples, the whole bit.

CALEB

Gentlemen, let me show you what we've developed for this mission *(Proudly pulls out a small black box.)*: the little black box! It contains everything you will need: computer, GPS, spy gizmos, sampling equipment and so on. Just push the UnZip Expander button on the side—

© 2004 Gospel Light. Permission to photocopy granted. *Raising Up Spiritual Champions*

JOSHUA *(Grabs box.)* DON'T touch that button! Our current version of ZipIt is COMPLETELY prehistoric. We'll NEVER get it all back in there!

SPIES *(In whiny-voiced unison.)* Oh, NO! This means trouble!

CALEB Just trust me. It works.

MOSES Enough of this technological ballyhoo. *(Pointing.)* GO!

All exit except Moses.
SCENE 2:
Forty days later.

MOSES *(Looking worried.)* Where are those spies? It's been 40 days! I thought they'd be back by now!

Spies *enter, moaning and sighing.* Moses *lowers sign as they move toward him, carrying grapes between or among them.* Caleb *and* Joshua *follow* Spies.

SPIES *(In whiny-voiced unison.)* MOSES! We've got trouble!

MOSES What do you mean? Those grapes look WONDERFUL! May I try one? *(Pretends to take a bite from a grape.)* Delicious! And one grape can serve a family for a WEEK!

SPIES *(In whiny-voiced unison.)* If you think the GRAPES are big, you should see the PEOPLE! They're GIANTS!

CALEB *(Saluting.)* Sir, our equipment worked perfectly. Each computer contains a detailed report. But to give you a summary, the land flows with milk and honey!

© 2004 Gospel Light. Permission to photocopy granted. *Raising Up Spiritual Champions*

JOSHUA *(Saluting.)* Sir! The military report, sir. Many cities are fortified. Walls, often very tall. Some of the people are quite tall, too. But we can TAKE them, sir!

SPIES *(In whiny-voiced unison.)* No WAY! These guys are SO BIG, we look like GRASSHOP-PERS beside them. They wear ARMOR! They have big, scary SWORDS. They have bad TEETH! They keep tigers as PETS! They have—

CALEB *(Interrupting.)* Cut it out, you whiners! Moses, we should go and take the land. We can DO IT!

SPIES *(In whiny-voiced unison.)* NOOOOO! We'll DIEEE!

JOSHUA *(Shaking his head.)* I'm gonna go make some mashed potatoes—to go with all this CHICKEN!

© 2004 Gospel Light. Permission to photocopy granted. *Raising Up Spiritual Champions*

What Happened Next? Cards

What did Moses do and say?

Read Numbers 14:5,19

What did Caleb and Joshua do and say, and what were the results?

Read Numbers 14:6-9,24,30

What did the 10 Spies say and do?

Read Numbers 13:31-32

What did the Israelites do and say, and what were the results?

Read Numbers 14:2-4,30

What did God say?

Read Numbers 14:26-30

© 2004 Gospel Light. Permission to photocopy granted. *Raising Up Spiritual Champions*

Distraction! Cards

Walk around this table on tiptoe.
Then crawl through the space under the table.

Jump over the broomstick five times.
Then tap your nose three times.

Slide your feet all the way around the hula hoop. Then step inside it and rub your tummy and pat your head.

Walk backwards around this chair
while touching it with only one finger.

Walk along this yarn like a tightrope.
Then bow three times.

© 2004 Gospel Light. Permission to photocopy granted. *Raising Up Spiritual Champions*

Verse Cards

Matthew
6:25,33

Matthew
7:12

Romans
8:26

Romans
8:28

Romans
15:7

Philippians
4:6-7

1 Thessalonians
5:18

James 1:5

© 2004 Gospel Light. Permission to photocopy granted. *Raising Up Spiritual Champions*

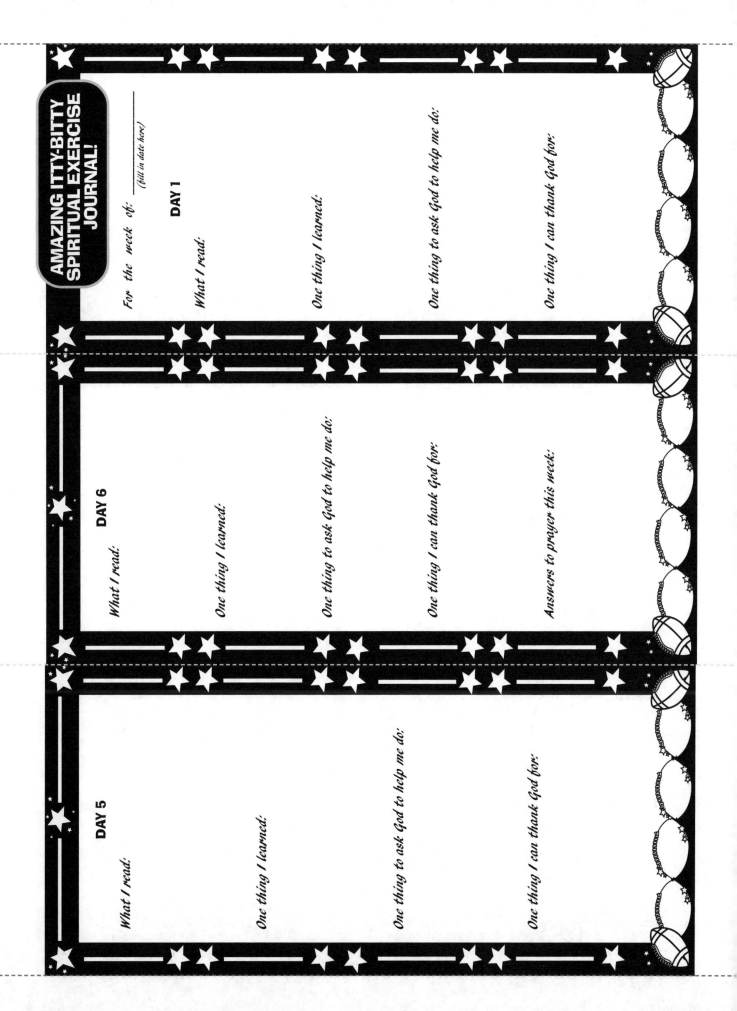

AMAZING ITTY-BITTY SPIRITUAL EXERCISE JOURNAL!

For the week of: _____
(fill in date here)

DAY 1

What I read:

One thing I learned:

One thing to ask God to help me do:

One thing I can thank God for:

DAY 6

What I read:

One thing I learned:

One thing to ask God to help me do:

One thing I can thank God for:

Answers to prayer this week:

DAY 5

What I read:

One thing I learned:

One thing to ask God to help me do:

One thing I can thank God for:

© 2004 Gospel Light. Permission to photocopy granted. *Raising Up Spiritual Champions*

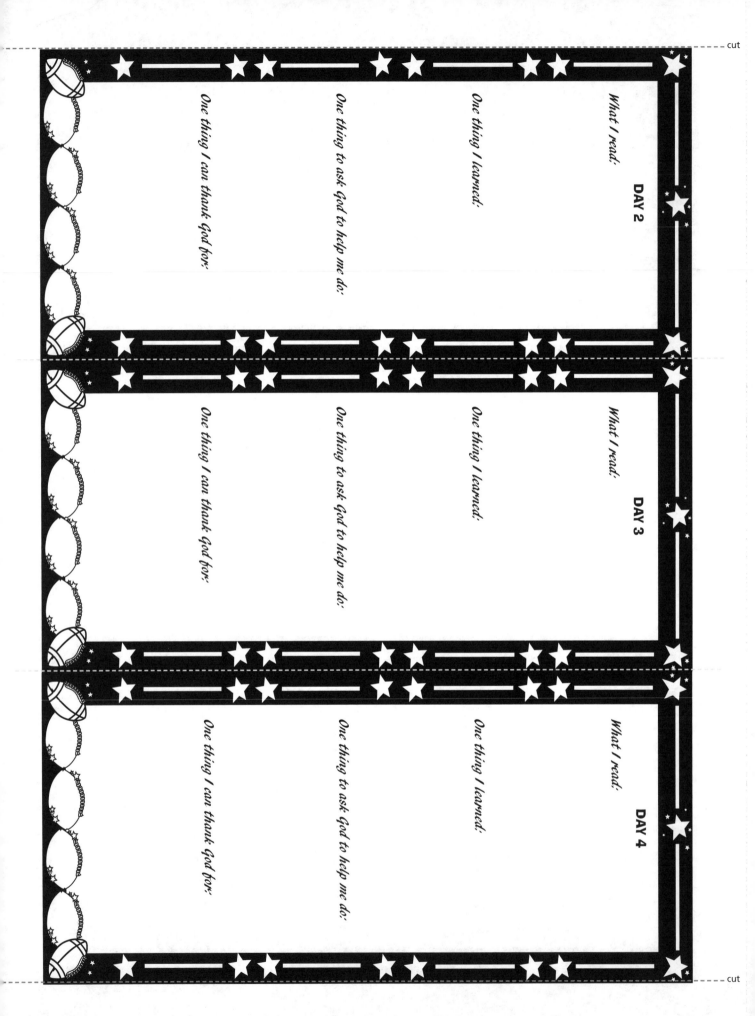

cut

DAY 2

What I read:

One thing I learned:

One thing to ask God to help me do:

One thing I can thank God for:

DAY 3

What I read:

One thing I learned:

One thing to ask God to help me do:

One thing I can thank God for:

DAY 4

What I read:

One thing I learned:

One thing to ask God to help me do:

One thing I can thank God for:

cut

© 2004 Gospel Light. Permission to photocopy granted. *Raising Up Spiritual Champions*

Where Do I Go for Answers?

The Write Stuff

Look at the Challenges and Bible Verse posters. While you were talking about the challenges, which two Bible verses seemed to you to be the most helpful? In each space below, write a challenge, the Bible verse reference and why you thought it was helpful.

Challenge 1:

The Bible Verse Reference:

Why I Thought It Was Helpful:

Challenge 2:

The Bible Verse Reference:

Why I Thought It Was Helpful:

Here are all of the Bible verse references from the Bible Verse poster. Use them next week for your spiritual exercise journal!

Matthew 6:25,33
Matthew 7:12
Romans 8:26
Romans 8:28

Romans 15:7
Philippians 4:6-7
1 Thessalonians 6:18
James 1:5

© 2004 Gospel Light. Permission to photocopy granted. *Raising Up Spiritual Champions*

THE CHALLENGE

This session's Bible Memory Verse:

"Stand firm. Let nothing move you. Always give yourself fully to the work of the Lord." 1 Corinthians 15:58

Bible Memory Verse repeated.
Coach's initials

Session 5 page completed.
Coach's initials

The Amazing Itty-Bitty Spiritual Exercise Journal is your BIG challenge of the week. Every day, read one of the verses listed on the other side. (You may choose to read more of each passage if you like!) Complete the journal page for that day. It's EXERCISE! It's like PRACTICING an important SKILL—not always EASY, but WORTH IT!

Did it!
Parent's initials

Family Challenge

Take one or more physical fitness walks together this week—around the block, to the park down the road. It doesn't have to be long. While you walk . . .

Talk About: Your personal spiritual fitness walk!

🖊 At what age or during what time in your life did you begin praying or reading the Bible as a regular part of your life?

🖊 What part of the Bible do you like best? What's the hardest part for you? Why?

🖊 What's your usual way to put God's Word into your heart and mind as the day begins? When seems to be the best time in the day for you to pray?

🖊 What is the easiest way for you to memorize God's Word?

Answer as many questions as you can. The important thing is for your whole family to grow and improve in the ability to stand firm in knowing and obeying God's Word!

Imagination Questions: What's the best part about knowing and spending time with your heavenly Father? If you could memorize only one part of the Bible, what part do you think you would memorize? When you get to heaven, what do you think God will say made Him happiest about you?

Did it!
Parent's initials

© 2004 Gospel Light. Permission to photocopy granted. *Raising Up Spiritual Champions*

Where Do I Go for Answers?

Session 5
Parent Page

For more information about this week's question, read Numbers 13:1-2,17-33; 14:1-10, the sources for our Bible study. You may also read Joshua 1:9; 1 Corinthians 16:13; 2 Thessalonians 2:15.

Tough Times, Tough Questions

We'd all like for our children to pass through childhood without the emotional scars caused by painful events. But it is not likely that our children will escape pain. Pain and loss come even to a happy child's life: death of a loved one, divorce, loss of a friend, separation from family members—the list of possible losses is long.

These losses give rise to the kinds of questions that are not easy to answer. *Why did Grandma die? Is it my fault you got divorced? Why did God let that person hurt my friend? Why didn't God stop this bad thing from happening? Doesn't He love us?*

Many of us have been taught not to discuss painful issues or to protect our children from pain by not talking about it. That is not only impossible, but it is also unhealthy! Hard as it may be to answer tough questions and to walk through painful times, "stuffing" our questions and feelings will not make them easier to deal with at a later date. Stuffing our pain is like holding a beach ball underwater. We can hold it for a while, but we grow tired of the effort. And eventually it pops up unexpectedly to hurt us and those close to us.

Because bad things do happen, we all must eventually face pain and its tough questions. The best thing we can do for our children is to teach them how to deal effectively with

life's tough issues. We can do this first through our own example and then through passing on what we've learned. As they learn from us, our children can move through the grief to effective healing and also gain the tools that will help them respond to loss and pain in healthy ways later on.

To best help our children, we need to first look at what our parents believed about tough times and tough questions. *Did my family talk about difficult issues? How did my parents equip me to deal with pain, loss and anger? What helped me to gain understanding of tough times when I was a child?* Remember that every new loss we experience brings back to mind other losses we

---

© 2004 Gospel Light. Permission to photocopy granted. *Raising Up Spiritual Champions*

have had. As we take time to evaluate our own losses and responses, we are better able to see what new tools and strategies we need to learn and use to help both ourselves and our children. Draw a time line of your own childhood to help you think about this.

Here are tips to help you and your child talk about difficult questions and painful issues as you walk through them together:

🖋 Recognize that grief is a natural reaction to any loss, whether one as simple as a poor grade in school or as serious as the death of a family member. Grieving may leave us in shock or confusion. We may not be able to concentrate. We may deny what we truly feel, or we may feel and express tremendous anger, sadness or guilt. We may forget to eat or may want to eat or to sleep all the time. We may feel hopeless. But our goal is to talk honestly with our children about their (and our) feelings, review the relationship we had with what we lost and then begin to gain understanding, acceptance and the ability to adapt to the new situation.

🖋 Lead the way. Our own honest words will model to a child how to express the feelings that come. Rather than ask, "How are you doing since Grandpa died?" try a simple statement that reveals how you really feel. This opens the door for your child to respond. "I still miss Grandpa a lot. I am sad that he won't be here to light the Christmas fire this year. What is something you miss about him?"

🖋 Listen to what your child says. Don't correct or explain. Listen.

🖋 Acknowledge how your child feels and accept your child's feelings. "It sounds like you're angry that you didn't get to say good-bye. I understand how that could make you mad. It doesn't seem fair." Then gently share your feelings. "I think I am mostly mad that I don't have my dad anymore. I still need him. Maybe it's silly, but I feel like he should have asked me first!"

🖋 Let your child know it is OK to cry and to express anger, fear, abandonment or sadness. It is even OK to express those feelings to God. (Look at the psalms David wrote. He was honest with God about his emotions!)

🖋 As much as we'd sometimes like to deny it, there are no easy answers to life's tough questions. Ironically, an adult's easy answer can shut down the chance to talk honestly with a child. We must curb the urge to speak for God to tell a child why something happened. We might offer a guess, an opinion, a feeling. But as one wise person said, "The question to ask is not Why? but What should we do about it?"

🖋 Our task is to help our children (and ourselves) move through the pain. Answers may come over time or they may never come. But we can say that because we know God loves us, we can wholeheartedly trust Him. We can be sure He cares and grieves with us. We can be thankful that no matter how bad the situation, He knows all about it. He says He is working on the problem right now, working it together for His glory and for our good—no matter how things look (see Romans 8:28).

Tough times will come. You may find that you are consumed with your own grief. But take time to be gentle with yourself and your child. Tell in an appropriate way the truth about how you feel. Ask questions that leave the door open for your child to tell his or her feelings. Don't try to tough it out! Instead, walk together through the tough times. Cry together and pray together. Go outdoors to yell, run or hike together. But do it together.

© 2004 Gospel Light. Permission to photocopy granted. *Raising Up Spiritual Champions*

Why Do I Need Other Christians?

6 Session

The Coach's Corner

While watching a recent NBA game someone asked, "How many NBA teams really play together as a team instead of as a mere supporting cast to one or two star players?" The estimate? Only about a third of the teams! Of course, NBA teams are built to make money. In professional sports (as in many other areas of life) true teamwork is easily subverted because the tendency is for players to do their best to become the star players, not to help others on the team!

But God did not design His family, the Body of Christ, to be a team like that of most of the NBA! Jesus (the ultimate superstar, completely worthy of our total, loyal support) showed us what kind of team He would build. Philippians 2 describes how He laid aside His superstar status to humble Himself completely to serve the lowest—us. Through the power of His death and resurrection, He created the ultimate *t-e-a-m*: people who *t*each, encourage, *a*ssist and *m*entor each other in His Body.

Barnabas was Jesus' kind of *t-e-a-m* member. He probably *t*aught Paul far more than we'll ever know this side of heaven, both by word and example. He was such a great encourager that we forget his name—Joseph, a Levite from Cyprus (see Acts 4:36)—but call him by his nickname, Son of Encouragement! When there was need, he *a*ssisted—giving his finances to those in need. And he *m*entored John Mark when Paul seemed to have given up on the young man so that John Mark could become useful to Paul in God's work. Barnabas's effective *t-e-a-m*work has touched all of Christianity and history since his lifetime!

Few of us will ever join an NBA team, but we can be the kind of *team* members who set aside our individual star agendas to become "completely humble and gentle" (Ephesians 4:2). That prepares us to follow Jesus to genuine victory!

Bible Memory Verse

"Therefore encourage one another and build each other up, just as in fact you are doing." 1 Thessalonians 5:11

Scripture Study

Acts 4:36-37; 9:26-30; 11:22-26; 15:36-40

Aims:

1. To discover that each part of the Body of Christ is important and needed so that other Christians can grow strong and healthy

2. To identify characteristics of the Body of Christ

3. To participate in activities to encourage other Christians

© 2004 Gospel Light. Permission to photocopy granted. *Raising Up Spiritual Champions*

Session Game Plan

WARM-UP (10-20 minutes)

Materials: Masking tape, sheet of butcher paper, marker.

Procedure: Small groups are assigned parts of the human body and make a case for why those parts are the most important.

POWER-UP (20-30 minutes)

Materials: Bible for each team member, four copies of "Without You!" (pp. 141-143), masking tape, sheet of butcher paper, marker.

Procedure: Read or act out a skit describing Barnabas's effect on others and list the characteristics of the Body of Christ displayed in his life.

PRACTICE (20-30 minutes)

Materials: Bible and *Session 6 Student Page* (pp. 145-146) for each team member, masking tape, Characteristics poster made during Power-Up, several Bible concordances (may be included in Bibles), index cards, markers in a variety of colors, pencils.

Procedure: Small groups formed earlier play a game to assign characteristics of the Body of Christ and then find Bible verses to help them understand that characteristic. Each team member completes side one of *Session 6 Student Page* and chooses a service project.

RALLY (10-20 minutes)

Materials: *Champions Music* CD and player, each team member's *Session 6 Student Page*, *Session 6 Parent Page* (pp. 147-148) for each team member, pencils.

Procedure: Sing worship songs, talk about the week's assignment and pray together.

© 2004 Gospel Light. Permission to photocopy granted. *Raising Up Spiritual Champions*

WARM-UP (10-20 minutes)

Materials: Masking tape, sheet of butcher paper, marker.

WHAT'S MOST IMPORTANT?

Make My Case!

Preparation: Tape butcher paper to wall. Write "What's Most Important?" across the top of butcher paper and then list the following body-part pairs: arm and elbow, wrist and hand, back and shoulder, foot and ankle, leg and knee.

Procedure: Help team members form pairs, trios or other small groups by finding similarities in clothing style, hair color, eye color, etc. **We're forming teams for today's debate. To get into a debate team, find (two people wearing shoes the same color) as yours.** Assign each debate team one of the body-part pairs listed on butcher paper. **A debate is where each team thinks of all the reasons why their opinions are correct. Then they try to convince others by making a good case, or argument!** Debate teams work together to build a case that their assigned body parts are more important to the body than the other parts listed (remind them to include demonstrations as well as words). **When your debate team is ready to present your case, move the body parts you were assigned!**

To help teams begin to build their cases, ask:

🖊 **What do these body parts do by themselves?**

🖊 **How do they help other parts function?**

🖊 **What's special about your parts of the body?**

Debate teams then take turns to stand, tell and demonstrate reasons the parts they were assigned are more important than the other parts. Next to the body parts on the poster, write comments or reasons as they are presented. After cases are presented, ask:

🖊 **How many of you have ever broken an (arm)?**

🖊 **What things couldn't you do while your (arm) was broken?**

🖊 **How did you feel when you could not (throw a ball)?**

🖊 **Which of the body parts listed do you think you could lose and still live?**

🖊 **God's Word describes us as being part of the Body of Christ. What do you think the Bible means by this?**

Conclusion: Each debate team did a great job of trying to convince us why its parts of the body are important. But we know that every part matters! Those of you who have broken an arm or a leg told us how difficult it is not to have all your body's parts working properly!

In every human body, billions of cells live together and work together. Every cell has a part to play. When a cell is healthy, it does the work it is supposed to do. All those healthy cells together make a strong, healthy body! Each member of God's family is like a cell or a part of a body. Each of us is important and together we are the Body of Christ. When each of us grows strong in knowing God, the Body of Christ is strong and healthy! Offer to talk with any team member who has questions about his or her decision to be a part of the Body of Christ (see "Leading a Student to Christ" on p. 39).

If your class has a disabled member, be loving and sensitive. Don't turn the spotlight on a disabled team member, but realize that pretending a disability doesn't exist is just as glaring. Instead, talk to the child before this session and let him or her know what will be talked about in this session. Then take your cue from the disabled team member. If he or she wants to participate and contribute information related to how the human body works, great! If a child is reluctant to participate, be careful not to pressure the child to go beyond what he or she feels comfortable sharing.

POWER-UP (20-30 minutes)

Materials: Bible for each team member, four copies of "Without You!" (pp. 141-143), masking tape, sheet of butcher paper, marker.

Preparation: Tape butcher paper to wall and label it "Characteristics." Distribute copies of "Without You!" to four team members to practice ahead of time.

Procedure: Be sure each team member has a Bible. **We're going to hear from some people who didn't know what they might have done without one man in the Bible. Let's listen to see if we can guess the person they are talking about!**

Four team members read skit aloud. After skit, let team members guess whom the skit was about. **We're going to brainstorm words that describe this member of the Body of Christ named Barnabas!** As team members suggest descriptive words, write them on Characteristics poster. (Note: Poster will be used later in the session.)

☺ **What are some words people in the skit used to describe Barnabas?**

☺ **What characteristics might Sarah, the widow from Jerusalem, say Barnabas showed to her?** (Kindness. Generosity. Love. Unselfishness. Giving.)

☺ **What qualities of character do you think Paul would say Barnabas had?** (Kindness. Protectiveness. Patience. Courage. Helpfulness. Compassion. Love. Faith.)

☺ **John Mark's life was changed because of Barnabas. What might he say were Barnabas's**

 © 2004 Gospel Light. Permission to photocopy granted. *Raising Up Spiritual Champions*

characteristics? (Kind. Patient. Believed in him. Trusted God. Was not afraid to do what he believed was right even when Paul disagreed.)

Conclusion: We've listed words that tell how the skit characters described Barnabas. But Barnabas was only one person, one cell in the Body of Christ. Who are some other people in the Body of Christ that these words describe? (*Volunteers name people from the Bible or from their own lives.*)

Our next challenge is to find Bible verses to help us understand the ways we work best together in the Body of Christ.

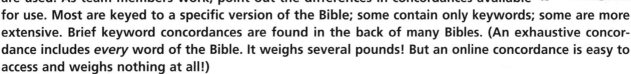

A Smart Start with Concordances!

Using a concordance is a helpful Bible-study skill. A concordance is a list of words used in the Bible. Each word is listed with references to places in the Bible where those words are used. As team members work, point out the differences in concordances available for use. Most are keyed to a specific version of the Bible; some contain only keywords; some are more extensive. Brief keyword concordances are found in the back of many Bibles. (An exhaustive concordance includes *every* word of the Bible. It weighs several pounds! But an online concordance is easy to access and weighs nothing at all!)

PRACTICE (20-30 minutes)

1. Hop to It!

Materials: Bible for each team member, masking tape, Characteristics poster made during Power-Up, several Bible concordances (may be included in Bibles), index cards, markers in a variety of colors.

Preparation: Lay a masking-tape line at the side of the room farthest from the Characteristics poster. Place concordances on a table in the center of the playing area. (If concordances are keyed to different versions of the Bible, keep a concordance for each version with a Bible of the same version.)

© 2004 Gospel Light. Permission to photocopy granted. *Raising Up Spiritual Champions*

Procedure: Team members re-form debate teams from Warm-Up. Distribute one index card for every characteristic listed on the poster, making sure that each team receives an equal number of cards. Each team takes a different color of marker and then team members stand behind the masking-tape line. At your signal, first member of each team takes marker, hops on one foot to the Characteristics poster and draws a line through one word listed to accept that word assignment for the team. Player returns to team, passes marker to next team member and play continues until all words are crossed out. Teams copy each word crossed out in their team's color onto a separate index card. **We're ready for our next challenge!**

2. Concordance Challenge

Procedure: Each small group takes a concordance and a Bible from the table. **With your team, find each of the words on your cards in a concordance. Then find a Bible verse that will help us understand how we use these characteristics to work better together in the Body of Christ.**

The verse you find might tell about a member of the Body of Christ who showed that characteristic. It might tell how we can show that characteristic. Or the verse might simply tell us to show the characteristic to others. When you find a verse you think will help us, copy the reference onto the blank side of the card. Find the verse and then use the card to mark it in your Bible.

Help team members use the concordances and find verses that are appropriate. Explain that the words in a concordance are in alphabetical order and the verses are listed in Bible order. Encourage teams to cooperate and help each other as they look for verses.

✎ **If you cannot find your word listed in the concordance, what word could you find that means the same thing?** (Invite team members to brainstorm synonyms for a word if a concordance doesn't match the version of the Bible used.)

After all teams have found verses, group teams together. A member of each team reads aloud the verses the team found and tells how the verses give help in understanding the characteristics. Group member then tapes top of index card with reference onto the Characteristics poster near the characteristic listed.

Now let's brainstorm ways you could show each characteristic your team found in the Bible. Teams brainstorm and then tell ways that they could show each characteristic.

Conclusion: The actions you've described are good ways to show how the Body of Christ works best together! Each of you have different abilities—things you like doing or are good at—that you can use to help the Body of Christ be strong and healthy as we all grow strong in becoming disciples of Jesus.

To simplify this activity, instruct teams to look only for New Testament verses. If your group is small or time is limited, choose four or five of the characteristics listed and find verses relating only to these. You may also choose to delete the Hop to It! portion of this Practice time and simply let teams choose index cards from a bag or other container.

© 2004 Gospel Light. Permission to photocopy granted. *Raising Up Spiritual Champions*

3. Playbook Preparation

Materials: *Session 6 Student Page* (pp. 145-146) for each team member, Characteristics poster, pencils.

Procedure: Distribute *Student Pages* and pencils to team members. Team members complete "The Write Stuff" by choosing characteristics and Bible verses from the index cards on the Characteristics poster. Invite volunteers to tell:

🏉 **Which characteristic(s) did you choose?**

🏉 **What is a way you can put that characteristic into action this week?**

🏉 **What kind of service project could you do to show this characteristic?**

Check-Off Time: Team members who completed *Session 5 Student Pages* may show completed pages to you and recite the previous week's Bible Memory Verse during this time. As time permits, talk with team members about their at-home work. **Where did you keep your journal at home? What was the best time of day to work on your journal? What was easy or hard about keeping up with the journal? What questions do you have about the verses you read?**

Seventh-Inning Stretch for Service!

One of the purposes of this session is to help team members understand ways the Body of Christ works together. The service projects that team members will be asked to complete as part of their *Student Page* assignment are designed to encourage each other and build each other up.

RALLY (10-20 minutes)

Worship: Sing "Teamwork" from *Champions Music* CD. **The Body of Christ can be called by many names.** Invite team members to tell several names. (The Church. God's family.) **This song says we're on God's team. That's another way to describe the Body of Christ!** Encourage team members to create motions for the song. Repeat song several times. Then sing "I Want to Follow Jesus."

Ask about answers to last week's prayer requests. Share a reason to praise God or a prayer request and then invite team members to share their requests. Team members may write prayer requests in the margins of their *Student Pages*.

Invite team members to close their eyes and ask volunteers to say aloud the characteristics that they have chosen to show during the week. **Whatever characteristic we plan to show, we can only**

Materials: *Champions Music* CD and player, each team member's *Session 6 Student Page*, *Session 6 Parent Page* (pp. 147-148) for each team member, pencils.

do it with God's help. Let's ask God to help us. Team members may pray sentence prayers aloud. Conclude by asking for God's help to be His disciples and thanking Him for the Body of Christ, the best team on Earth! (Optional: Coaches lead groups of 8 to 12 team members each in prayer time. If you started a record of prayer requests during earlier sessions, refer to it during this prayer time.)

Wrap-Up: Look at both sides of the *Student Page* with team members, pencils in hand. Be sure they understand the assignments on side two. Invite questions about assignments. **Doing the service project will be one way you can show the characteristic of the Body of Christ you chose. Enjoy it and be creative!** Be sure every team member leaves with his or her *Student Page* and *Parent Page*.

© 2004 Gospel Light. Permission to photocopy granted. *Raising Up Spiritual Champions*

Without You!

Based on Acts 4:36-37; 9:26-30; 11:22-26; 15:36-40

CHARACTERS:

KELLY GREEN, a talk-show host who talks grandly and applauds often

SARAH, a widow from the Early Church in Jerusalem

PAUL, a cranky persecutor turned well-known apostle

JOHN MARK, a young man from Jerusalem

I'm Kelly Green. Welcome to today's edition of *Without You!*—where we discover the CONSEQUENCES of one person's actions, and YOU, our audience, guess our mystery person's identity! Our guests today come from around the Roman Empire. Our first guest is Sarah, of Jerusalem. She has quite a story to tell about CONSEQUENCES! Welcome, Sarah! *(Applauds.)*

Thank you, Kelly. It's true—this IS quite a story! After my husband died, I was SO sad! And I had no hope. I was selling my furniture to buy food. When that money was gone, I expected to STARVE to death. But then I joined God's family. And WHAT a wonderful new family! People shared with each other. I had food every day! But one day, we heard the food was running out. The same awful feeling of fear and hopelessness came back. What would we DO? But then—HE showed up!

What did our mystery man DO? Tell us, Sarah. We're all ears!

He sold an EXPENSIVE piece of land. He made a LOT of money! He could have kept the land OR the money for himself. But instead, he gave it ALL—a big BAG of money—to God's family. Without HIM, we might have STARVED!

Thank you, Sarah. *(Applauds.)* Our next guest is world famous—but he'll share some NOT-so-famous information about our mystery man! Please welcome with me Paul the apostle! *(Applauds.)*

Thank you, Kelly. I'll be glad to tell a few stories about our mystery man. Very quiet about what he does, very quiet. Likes to stay in the background, so to speak. But without HIM, I don't know where I'D be—or God's family, either!

© 2004 Gospel Light. Permission to photocopy granted. *Raising Up Spiritual Champions*

KELLY GREEN: Wow. This sounds serious, Paul. What happened?

PAUL: As most people know, I started out as a persecutor of God's family. I'm not proud of that! But one day, Jesus stopped me on the road to Damascus. My whole life changed! I began to tell people how Jesus is the Messiah! But not EVERYBODY believed I was changed. God's family in Jerusalem wanted nothing to do with me! When they heard I'd joined God's family, they figured it was a trick. They were still terrified of me! But then HE came to me.

KELLY GREEN: What did he DO, Paul? We want to hear the consequences!

PAUL: He took me under his wing, so to speak. Brought me with him to the leaders of the church in Jerusalem. Explained what had happened to me in Damascus. Because everyone loved and trusted our mystery man, they accepted me as well. If it hadn't been for his believing in me, I can't imagine how the REST of my story in God's family would have been written!

KELLY GREEN: I understand that was only the BEGINNING of your friendship!

PAUL: Indeed! Several years later our mystery man began to preach in Antioch and so MANY folks joined God's family, he needed HELP! So he came and found me. Took me back with him. We spent about a year teaching together. Saw LOTS more people join God's family! It was a great time!

KELLY GREEN: Thank you, Paul. We'll hear more from Paul in a moment. But now, another guest will add to the story of our mystery man. *(Applauds.)* Please welcome John Mark!

JOHN MARK: Thank you, Kelly! Great to be here! And Paul! Good to see you! Kelly, Paul is one of my greatest mentors—second only to our mystery man.

PAUL: *(To John Mark.)* Grand to see you too, son. *(To Kelly)* Kelly, truth be told, if it weren't for our mystery man, you'd probably never see the two of US together. You see, I have an awful temper. I disagreed with our mystery man so STRONGLY about this boy—

© 2004 Gospel Light. Permission to photocopy granted. *Raising Up Spiritual Champions*

JOHN MARK: Now, don't go making excuses for me, Paul. It was MY fault! I DID chicken out and go HOME! I sure caused you two a lot of grief.

PAUL: Ah, but God used it all for the best, didn't He? Because our mystery man believed in you, he took you with him. So I took Silas with me. And TWICE as much got done in God's family!

JOHN MARK: He sure did believe in me. He didn't give up on me—

PAUL: And I confess, I had. I was just plain stubborn. But in the end, I saw he was right. You've grown to be a great help to me, John Mark, and a great help to God's family all over the world!

JOHN MARK: Thanks, Paul. Without our mystery man, I don't know WHERE I'd have ended up!

KELLY GREEN: Thank you both. *(Applauds.)* This is MOST heartwarming! And now, ladies and gentlemen! It's time to ask—who IS this mystery man? This man without whom the family of God would have been in great need? This man who is a grand example of a healthy part of the Body of Christ! Can you guess his name? *(Pauses.)*

Here he IS—ladies and gentlemen, Joseph of Cyprus, better known as Barnabas, the Son of Encouragement! Missionary! Pastor! Friend! Mentor!

The Write Stuff

Look on the Characteristics poster to find at least one or two characteristics and Bible verses. Copy those characteristics and verses onto your paper.

What characteristic do you want to show this coming week? Draw a picture that reminds you of a way you can show that characteristic.

© 2004 Gospel Light. Permission to photocopy granted. *Raising Up Spiritual Champions*

THE CHALLENGE

This session's Bible Memory Verse:

"Therefore encourage one another and build each other up, just as in fact you are doing." 1 Thessalonians 5:11

Bible Memory Verse repeated.
Coach's initials

Session 6 page completed.
Coach's initials

Family Challenge

Each family member is challenged to do at least one action to encourage or build up each other this week! You don't need to keep a chart or check-list—just make a mental note!

This building up can be as simple as saying kind words. Or go big! Have a "you are special" day for each family member! Prepare that person's favorite meal or play a favorite game in that person's honor!

Talk About: What time of day is it hardest for us to encourage each other? How do you feel when (Susan) says kind words about you?

Imagination Question: What act of kindness would surprise you the most?

Did it!
Parent's initials

aka The Seventh-Inning Stretch (Service Project)

You may choose any service project that encourages another person and is approved ahead of time by an adult. But here are two ideas to start you thinking:

Secret Encourager! First, brainstorm some specific words of encouragement and Bible verses with an adult. **Second,** select a leader (pastor, Sunday School teacher, etc.) in your church to whom you'd like to send a secret encouragement message. **Third,** make and decorate a message or two, using those words and Bible verses you brainstormed. Dress up your messages with stamps, stickers, etc. Place your personalized message in an envelope, address it and give it to your coach next session to deliver anonymously for you!

Show Time! Do this with several other team members. **First,** arrange for a time with the teacher of a younger class when you may put on a puppet show for them. Ask that teacher to suggest a Bible story. **Second,** find the story in a children's Bible storybook and create simple puppets (paper-plate faces, sock puppets, etc.) for characters. **Third,** set up a time to practice your presentation by reading the story aloud and using the puppets to act out the story. **Fourth,** give your presentation at the agreed-upon time. Have fun!

Did it!
Parent's initials

© 2004 Gospel Light. Permission to photocopy granted. *Raising Up Spiritual Champions*

Why Do I Need Other Christians?

For more information about this week's question, read Acts 4:36-37; 9:26-30; 11:22-26; 15:36-40, the sources for our Bible study. You may also read Colossians 4:10; 2 Timothy 4:11.

Talk So That They Listen, Listen So That They Talk

Talking to children in ways that create under-standing and gain results may seem an elusive skill. *How does she get her kids to respond so quickly? What does he say that make his kids so loving toward him?* Although Good Communication with Your Own Children wasn't a class offered at most of our high schools, the opportunity to ace this subject is still available!

First, let's look at Jesus. When around children, He loved instead of lectured. He touched them and blessed them. He knew children need far more action than talk: Still developing their verbal skills, kids know that actions say far more than words do. Even when kids don't understand the meanings of all our words, they quickly grasp the emotional content of what we say. Also notice how Jesus talked about and physically held children up as examples for adults to follow. He showed that He valued children! When children are certain that we value them, they are far more open with us.

Second, let's consider the old truth "People don't care how much you know until they know how much you care." Even with our own children, the basis for good communication is genuine relationship. Relationship is most easily built by listening! That means we have to ask good questions and listen without criticizing to our children! Ask open-ended questions that have no right or wrong or one-word answers. (Instead of, "Did you have a good day?" try, "What was the best part of your day?" or "On a scale of 1 to 10, how would you rate your day? Why?") Then let your child talk without

© 2004 Gospel Light. Permission to photocopy granted. *Raising Up Spiritual Champions*

feeling criticized. When our kids realize it's safe to move beyond one-word answers and talk freely, they will have plenty to say!

Third, remember that good communication goes beyond basic housekeeping issues ("Did you feed the dog? Where is the tape?"). Find a common interest beyond household affairs. It may be a hobby or activity you both enjoy. If needed, read bits of a newspaper or magazine aloud to each other and ask "what do you think?" kinds of questions. Read a book aloud to each other and talk about the characters' actions. Talk about a TV show you watched together. (Stick to aspects of the show that will not make your child wary of giving an opinion. Avoid emotionally charged subjects at first to avoid shutting down the conversation!)

How to Talk Effectively

◆ Listen to your child with the same respect you would show an adult. (This can be tough to do, but keep practicing!) Resist the urge to interrupt, finish a thought, put down or talk down!

◆ Listen without criticizing your child's words. (Children process their ideas as they are talking. If a child's words seem off base, wait, listen more and ask questions.)

◆ Use your child's name often. (A child may well assume you are *not* talking to him or her unless you use the child's name!)

◆ Use touch to express your love as you talk.

◆ Frequently model the kinds of caring words you want your child to say: "Please," "I'm sorry," "That's all right," "I understand," "Thank you."

◆ Be quick to see and point out what is good. Your child's openness and confidence blossom when he or she hears you say, "I see . . ." and "I appreciate . . ."

The Killers of Conversation

◆ Correcting what you *think* your child is saying or finishing a sentence or thought.

◆ Negative nonverbal actions (sighing, looking away, glancing at your watch). If you are taking the steps described above, you will have no time to behave negatively!

◆ Sarcasm. Sarcasm is always based on the idea "I'm smarter than you." Your child will likely feel belittled by your tone of voice alone.

◆ Overexplanation. Keep explanations short and to the point.

◆ Exaggeration. Children are very sensitive to a parent's level of honesty. Part of our work as parents is to help our kids understand how the world works. Don't confuse or abuse their trust by exaggerating or telling them anything untrue. Take the power of your own words seriously!

◆ Name-calling shuts down open communication. When there is a problem, focus on the behavior, not the child. Help your child know how to correct problem behavior by giving choices and positive directions. Labeling puts a question in your child's mind as to whether or not you value him or her.

Remember that every time you talk with your child, you have the option to communicate God's love to him or her in some way—or not. Cultivate a loving relationship with your child through your conversation!

ADDED BONUS SUGGESTION:
Try all of these ideas with your spouse!

© 2004 Gospel Light. Permission to photocopy granted. *Raising Up Spiritual Champions*

How Do I Plan to Grow as a Disciple? Review and Personal Discipleship Planning

7
Session

The Coach's Corner

In his book *Transforming Children into Spiritual Champions*, George Barna notes that ministering to children is about perseverance: "continual and progressive investments for many consecutive years."[1] Because of society's short-term, microwave-ready mind-set, it can be easy to expect a short discipleship course to manufacture a result of imminent Christian maturity! But a biblical growth pattern differs widely from the timetable for a manufactured product: A planted seed sprouts and grows. It requires those "continual and progressive investments" of nurturing rain and sunlight over time until fruit is borne and maturity is seen.

We all know how exhilarating it can be to start a new project—and we all know how difficult it is to be faithful and remain consistent in doing what is right when it's far less exciting than short-term results and less glamorous than splashy effects. Yet over the course of our lives our faithful, consistent time and attention are what exhibits the love of Christ to a child.

This week your team members will focus on their personal discipleship plans. Perhaps we'd be wise to make discipleship plans of our own! We need to plan ways to challenge ourselves to grow to spiritual maturity. But we also need to make solid plans for ways to help these team members, with whom we've built relationships, grow into wholehearted followers of Jesus. It could be lunch with the team once a month. It might be a phone call every few weeks. But planned ongoing attention and consistent contact will grow relationships that keep the *t-e-a-m* (*t*each, *e*ncourage, *a*ssist, *m*entor) spirit going! (Note: For ideas to help you continue your coaching relationships, see page 24.)

Note

1. George Barna, *Transforming Children into Spiritual Champions* (Ventura, CA: Regal Books, 2003), p. 120.

Bible Memory Verse

"Just as you received Christ Jesus as Lord, continue to live in him, rooted and built up in him, strengthened in the faith as you were taught, and overflowing with thankfulness." Colossians 2:6-7

Aims:

1. To review the big picture of discipleship

2. To evaluate, reflect and make reminders of what we have learned

3. To complete a discipleship plan

© 2004 Gospel Light. Permission to photocopy granted. *Raising Up Spiritual Champions*

Session Game Plan

WARM-UP (10-20 minutes)

Materials: *Champions Music* CD and player, index cards, marker, sheet of butcher paper, masking tape.

Procedure: Play a review game to help talk about what it means to follow Jesus and describe concepts team members have learned.

POWER-UP (20-30 minutes)

Materials: *Session 7 Student Page* (pp. 161-162) for each team member, Say What? (pp. 157-159), scissors, masking tape, posters from Sessions 1-6, pencils, lunch bags, station items (see p. 153).

Procedure: Team members move through stations to do activities in which they review and reflect on what they have learned.

PRACTICE (20-30 minutes)

Materials: Each team member's *Session 7 Student Page*, materials for personal reminders (see p. 155), pencils.

Procedure: Team members will make personal reminder items and use *Student Pages* to make personal discipleship plans.

RALLY (10-20 minutes)

Materials: *Champions Music* CD and player, each team member's *Session 7 Student Page*, *Session 7 Parent Page* (pp. 163-164) for each team member, pencils, personal reminder items made in Practice.

Procedure: Sing worship songs, talk about the week's assignment and pray together.

© 2004 Gospel Light. Permission to photocopy granted. *Raising Up Spiritual Champions*

WARM-UP (10-20 minutes)

Walk Like You

Materials: *Champions Music CD* and player, index cards, marker, sheet of butcher paper, masking tape.

Preparation: Number index cards 1-6, making one card for each team member. Draw a star beside the number on one card. Lay all cards on floor number-side down in a large circle. Tape butcher paper to wall. Draw a large body outline on the butcher paper.

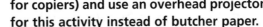

Photocopy a team member's photograph onto a blank transparency sheet (suitable for copiers) and use an overhead projector for this activity instead of butcher paper.

Procedure: Team members line up around outside of the circle of index cards, each player next to a card. **Our challenge is a little like the game we played in the first session. At my signal, secretly look at the card nearest you and then place card back down on floor. If there is a star on your card, you are the leader for the first round of this game. When the music starts, everyone walks around the circle (clapping hands). The leader will begin a new motion, so watch to imitate the actions of the person ahead of you. Soon everyone will be moving in the same way. When the music stops, freeze and tell me who the leader was!** Team members secretly check cards to see if he or she will lead the round. Play "I Want to Follow Jesus" from *Champions Music* CD as students move in circle. After 15-20 seconds, stop the music. Everyone freezes in place. Team members tell who the leader was. Repeat activity as time permits. Then answer one or more of the following questions:

● **Was it easy or hard to follow the leader? Why?**

● **Who are some everyday leaders we follow?**

● **What are some reasons people follow Jesus?**

● **What is a way a kid your age can show he or she follows Jesus?**

● **How can you help yourself to become a better follower of Jesus?**

● **What have you seen another person do that seems to help him or her be a better follower of Jesus?**

● **Describe a time when it is hard to follow Jesus.**

At the end of the discussion, each team member picks up the nearest card to discover at which numbered station he or she begins Power-Up.

Refer to the butcher paper sheet with the large body outline. (Optional: Give each team member a large sheet of paper on which to draw a body outline.) **We're going to use this outline to describe what we have learned a disciple is like.**

Point to head. **What words might describe what we've learned about a disciple's thoughts or mind?** Draw a thought balloon near the head and write team members' words inside it.

Point to heart area. **What words might describe the heart or feelings of a follower of Jesus?** Draw a large heart shape out to the side of the body shape. Write team members' words inside heart.

Point to hands or feet. **What words might describe a disciple's actions? What are some things a disciple does?** Write team members' words beside hands and feet outlines.

Conclusion: We've talked about reasons people follow Jesus. We've described a disciple. Now that we're warmed up and ready to go, look at the number on your index card. Move to the station numbered the same as your card!

To review in another way, form six small groups. Each group brainstorms and makes up a cheer or rap that tells the main idea of each of the first six sessions. (For words and ideas, refer to each session's title and posters.)

Groups practice the cheer or rap and then teach it to others or plan to share it with parents at next week's celebration time. (The Bible Memory Verses for each session may also be made into cheers or raps!)

POWER-UP (20-30 minutes)

Materials: *Session 7 Student Page* (pp. 161-162) for each team member, Say What? (pp. 157-159), scissors, masking tape, posters from Sessions 1-6, pencils, lunch bags, station items (see p. 153).

Preparation: Photocopy and cut apart Say What? pages. Tape each section beside the matching Session 1-6 posters, creating six stations around the room. Place a pencil and a *Session 7 Student Page* inside a lunch bag for each team member. (Note: If you are the only coach with a small group of team members, prepare at least two stations. If there are several coaches and small groups, lead this activity with all small groups together and prepare at least four stations. Assign a coach or other adult to each station.)

© 2004 Gospel Light. Permission to photocopy granted. *Raising Up Spiritual Champions*

ITEMS for each Say What? Station

(Note: Not all stations require materials.)

STATION 1: Sheets of paper and pens of different colors.

STATION 2: Chenille wires in a variety of sizes and colors.

STATION 3: Bibles, markers or pens for drawing.

STATION 4: Play dough or clay.

STATION 5: Audiocassette recorder and blank cassette or handheld video recorder and videocassette.

STATION 6: None. (Optional: A few simple costumes—hat, glasses, vest, etc.)

Procedure: Distribute a prepared bag to each team member. **Use the pencil in your bag to write your name on your bag. Take your bag with you so that you have your pencil and *Student Page* at each station.** Team members begin at the station number indicated on the index card they chose in Warm-Up and complete the assignment at as many Say What? stations as time permits. Initial *Student Pages* when station assignment is completed.

Conclusion: When all team members are close to completing the activities at each station say, You are showing in lots of creative ways what you remember about being disciples of Jesus! Next, we're going to make our plans for the coming week's challenge. Later, you'll each make a reminder for yourself of something important that you learned.

© 2004 Gospel Light. Permission to photocopy granted. *Raising Up Spiritual Champions*

PRACTICE (20-30 minutes)

1. Personal Planner

Materials: Each team member's *Session 7 Student Page*, pencils.

Procedure: Show side two of the *Student Page*. **Take your page from your bag. Let's look at the second side. It looks like a personal planner. Each of us will use this page to make a personal discipleship plan for the coming week. The challenge for the week is to complete the plan you make!** Team members follow directions on page to complete plans. They may talk to you or look at the Say What? stations to gather ideas for their personal plans.

2. Personal Reminder Project

Preparation: Place materials in the center of a table (prepare a table for every six to eight team members).

Materials: Markers, materials for personal reminders (see p. 155).

Procedure: To help team members plan reminders that will have meaning for each one, ask:

🏈 **Which of these colors might remind you of something you have learned about being disciples of Jesus or what you have planned to do to follow Him? Which of these items would you like to use to make a helpful reminder?**

🏈 **What kind of reminder might you most likely notice every day?**

🏈 **What might be something you could hang in your room? Wear? Hang on your doorknob?**

🏈 **What word or phrase can you add to remind you of following Jesus?**

Conclusion: While we make our personal discipleship reminders, we'll work silently. We are not going to talk. Having silent time gives us a chance to think and pray while we work. Make your reminder in any way you like. It doesn't matter how it looks. No one will ask you to tell about it. It's between you and God. The goal is for it to remind you of something important you have learned or something important you want to do to show that you follow Jesus! Each team member uses materials in any way to create a personal reminder of one or more plans made or ideas learned during the previous six sessions.

© 2004 Gospel Light. Permission to photocopy granted. *Raising Up Spiritual Champions*

Options for a variety of unique personal reminders:

Nature rubbings—paper, crayons and nature items

Nature collages—glue, nature items, card stock

Braids, wraps or ties—nature items (twigs, dried plants, etc.), yarn or embroidery floss

Construction or sculpture—nature items, glue, play dough or clay for bases

Sculptures—Play dough or clay (add beads and/or nature items as desired)

Reminder stones—river stones (can also decorate with glitter glue, and small items)

Bracelets or door hangers—chenille wires, yarn, beads, etc.

Scrapbooks or bookmarks—variety of paper, pens and decorative scissors

Providing a variety of these items and suggesting several ideas will likely spark creative and meaningful expressions!

3. Playbook Preparation

Check-Off Time: As team members finish their personal reminder items, those who completed *Session 6 Student Pages* may show their completed pages to you and recite the previous week's verse. As time permits, talk with team members about their at-home work. **What did you enjoy most about the challenge you completed? What's another way you can think of to encourage someone else?**

On to the Finish Line:

Planning for Next Week

The final session is quite different from the others: It is first a time of evaluation and second a time of celebration in which family members participate.

Plan the final session now so that you can properly prepare!

Your celebration can be simple or elaborate. The celebration can include food, decorations, displays, skits, songs, personal stories, a commitment ceremony and an awards ceremony. As you plan, customize the celebration to your group's needs and abilities.

An invitation for this celebration is part of this week's *Parent Page*. Be sure to reproduce enough *Parent Pages* for everyone to be invited! (Consider inviting the pastor, the children's pastor and/or team members' Sunday School teachers.) Be sure team members fill in the information in the blanks on the invitation.

© 2004 Gospel Light. Permission to photocopy granted. *Raising Up Spiritual Champions*

RALLY (10-20 minutes)

Materials: *Champions Music* CD and player, each team member's *Session 7 Student Page*, a *Session 7 Parent Page* (pp. 163-164) for each team member, pencils, personal reminder items made in Practice.

Worship: Sing one or two of the team members' favorite songs from the *Champions Music* CD. **Next week our families will be joining us for a celebration. We want to show our families what we have learned. Which songs should we sing next week? Let's vote!** Sing "I Want to Follow Jesus" together. (Optional: If team members have created motions for this song, allow time to practice the motions to prepare for presentation next week during the celebration time.)

Ask about answers to last week's prayer requests. Share a reason to praise God or a prayer request and then invite teammates to share their requests. Team members may write prayer requests in the margins of their *Student Pages*.

Close in prayer. **Thank You, God, for loving us and putting us on Your team. Thank You for helping us become the best followers of Jesus we can be. Please help each of us complete the plans we have made. Help us remember the ways in which we want to get better as followers of Jesus. In Jesus' name, amen.** (Optional: Coaches lead groups of 8 to 12 team members each in prayer time. If you started a record of prayer requests during earlier sessions, refer to it during this prayer time.)

Wrap Up: Look at side two of the *Student Page* with team members and answer questions about ways to complete the plans they have made. **We'll be eager to hear next week about what happens as you do what you have planned!** Assign team members a part in the preparation for next week's final celebration. Distribute *Parent Pages* at this time. **We need to prepare our invitations for next week!** Give or post the needed information so that team members can complete invitations. (Optional: Ask for volunteers to bring snacks and drinks and ask team members to fill in the appropriate place on their invitations. You may also want to confirm details with parents prior to Session 8.)

Invite team members to gather their Personal Reminder items. **Hold and look at your reminder item. Think about what you felt while you made it. This week, use it to remind you of what you have learned or decided as a follower of Jesus. Next week during our celebration, we will be recalling these ideas and our prayers about being Jesus' disciples.**

Be sure every team member leaves with his or her *Session 7 Student Page* and a completed invitation on the *Session 7 Parent Page*.

© 2004 Gospel Light. Permission to photocopy granted. *Raising Up Spiritual Champions*

Say What?

What Does It Mean to Be a Disciple?

1 Session

"Just as you received Christ Jesus as Lord, continue to live in him, rooted and built up in him, strengthened in the faith as you were taught, and overflowing with thankfulness."
Colossians 2:6-7

Choose one:

1 Dictate (say words to be written down by a coach) to complete this sentence: To me, following Jesus means . . .

2 Dictate words to answer this question: What is one way following Jesus has changed an action in my life?

The coach at this station will save the dictations to make a book.

What Is Most Important to Me?

2 Session

"Seek first his kingdom and his righteousness, and all these things will be given to you as well."
Matthew 6:33

Complete this sentence:

One way I can show I am putting God first is . . .

Then use chenille wires to make an item you could use to put God first (Bible, clock, money, etc.).

Say the completed sentence to a coach as you show and explain your chenille wire item. Place the item you made in your bag.

© 2004 Gospel Light. Permission to photocopy granted. *Raising Up Spiritual Champions*

How Does Knowing the Truth Make a Difference in My Life?

3
Session

"Show me your ways, O Lord, teach me your paths; guide me in your truth and teach me, for you are God my Savior, and my hope is in you all day long."
Psalm 25:4-5

Choose a verse from the Bible that you know. (Read Romans 12:9-18 for some ideas.) Then think of a way in which obeying that verse could change one thing you do. Draw a picture of that action.

Show and describe your picture to a coach.

What Happens When I Sin?

4
Session

"Have mercy on me, O God, according to your unfailing love; according to your great compassion blot out my transgressions. Wash away all my iniquity and cleanse me from my sin."
Psalm 51:1-2

Use play dough or clay to shape one of the following:

♛ A sculpture that reminds you of how you feel when you fail to obey God

♛ A sculpture that reminds you of how you feel when you know you are forgiven

♛ A sculpture that reminds you of a way you want God to help you change

Show and explain your finished sculpture to a coach. Leave the sculpture at the station.

© 2004 Gospel Light. Permission to photocopy granted. *Raising Up Spiritual Champions*

Where Do I Go for Answers?

5 Session

"Stand firm. Let nothing move you. Always give yourself fully to the work of the Lord."
1 Corinthians 15:58

Audio- or videotape yourself answering this question: What would you say to someone who is having a hard time trusting in God?

Be sure the recorder is working. A coach will hold the camera or microphone.

Why Do I Need Other Christians?

6 Session

"Therefore encourage one another and build each other up, just as in fact you are doing."
1 Thessalonians 5:11

Think of one way you could build up or encourage another person in the Body of Christ.

By yourself or with a friend, act out that way for a coach.

© 2004 Gospel Light. Permission to photocopy granted. *Raising Up Spiritual Champions*

How Do I Plan to Grow as a Disciple?

Say What?
Starting at the station with the number that matches your card, do each activity.
Ask a coach to sign below when you complete the activity.

1. You did it! _____ Coach's initials

2. You did it! _____ Coach's initials

3. Draw your picture in the space below. You did it! _____ Coach's initials

4. You did it! _____ Coach's initials

5. You did it! _____ Coach's initials

6. You did it! _____ Coach's initials

© 2004 Gospel Light. Permission to photocopy granted. *Raising Up Spiritual Champions*

This Session's Bible Memory Verse:

"Just as you received Christ Jesus as Lord, continue to live in him, rooted and built up in him, strengthened in the faith as you were taught, and overflowing with thankfulness." Colossians 2:6-7 (This should sound familiar!)

Bible Memory
Verse repeated.
Coach's initials

☐

Session 7
page completed.
Coach's initials

☐

3 ○ I will be in this place: _____
out the plans I have made.   to carry

Draw the place here.

4 ○ I will talk to an adult about my plan.
○ I did it!   _____ initials   _____ date

Family Challenge

Support your team member.

Talk About: How is *your* discipleship plan working?

Imagination Question: How would our family be different if each of us who is a disciple sticks to our discipleship plans?

Did It!
Parent's initials

☐

---

2 ○ I will keep a journal about what I read this week in the Bible. I will set aside _____ minutes per day (time) every day to carry out the plans I have made.

LAST MONTH

THIS MONTH

NEXT MONTH

Draw a smiley face each time you complete a day!

1

2

3

4

5

6

This Week:

1 ○ I will take time to look at and think about my reminder item. Then I will write down a prayer about what my reminder project means. Write your prayer here.

---

162 • Personal Planner!

© 2004 Gospel Light. Permission to photocopy granted. *Raising Up Spiritual Champions*

We want to CELEBRATE our accomplishments with you and ask
your help to INSPIRE us to keep on growing as disciples of Jesus!

Date:

Time:

Place:

Please Bring:

How Did I Do?
Evaluation and Celebration

8 Session

It's rarely difficult to motivate people to celebrate! The idea of celebration is used everywhere from advertising sales celebrations to encouraging us to overindulge ("Celebrate! You deserve it!"). But in *Merriam-Webster's Collegiate Dictionary* "celebrate" is defined as "observing a notable occasion with festivities."[1] Without a noted occasion or reason to celebrate, the festivities are drained of joy. They become empty and meaningless.

At the end of this course on discipleship, however, the real accomplishments involved in completing this course should be noted "with festivities." The focused work of every team member, parent and coach should indeed be celebrated! Such celebration creates community, which is a foundational part of discipleship. George Barna notes that community is "the final practice that we must facilitate for our children . . . engagement in a community of believers, where they are accepted, instructed, encouraged, supported and held accountable."[2] Celebrating together as a community of Jesus' followers tells young disciples that we are all in this together and we're eager to *teach*, encourage, *assist*, and *mentor* them into full maturity, because none of us is a superdisciple; we are all part of God's family. That's the kind of teamwork that will long outlive our short coaching careers. It's eternal investment that yields eternal results!

As you plan this celebration in community, take time to recognize and celebrate the ways you have all grown as disciples. Thank God both privately and publicly for what He has done through this time. As Paul said in Colossians 2:6-7, it is only as we live in Jesus, rooted and built up in Him, that we grow strong in our faith, overflow with thankfulness and become better able to nurture each other into becoming God's champions—wholehearted followers of Jesus!

Notes
1. *Merriam-Webster's Collegiate Dictionary*, 10th ed., s.v. "celebrate."
2. George Barna, *Transforming Children into Spiritual Champions* (Ventura, CA: Regal Books, 2003), p. 74.

BIBLE MEMORY VERSE

"Just as you received Christ Jesus as Lord, continue to live in him, rooted and built up in him, strengthened in the faith as you were taught, and overflowing with thankfulness." Colossians 2:6-7

Aims:

1. To display and communicate that being a disciple means to think and act like Jesus

2. To evaluate progress in learning about and acting as a disciple of Jesus

3. To celebrate individual and team accomplishments

© 2004 Gospel Light. Permission to photocopy granted. *Raising Up Spiritual Champions*

Session Game Plan

WARM-UP (10-15 minutes)

Materials: *Session 7 Student Page* (pp. 161-162) for each team member, brainstorming posters from Sessions 1-6, masking tape, poster board, markers.

Procedure: Team members check in with their coach to evaluate completion of the past week's plans and work together to create Big Idea posters using information from Session 1-6 posters. (Note: If parents will be present during Warm-Up, give them Letter Starters (p. 176) and writing materials. Parents begin writing letters to their children.)

POWER-UP (20-35 minutes)

Materials: Buddy Bingo! (p. 173), pencils, small prizes for winners.

Procedure: Family members enter the classroom and all play a game.

EXTENDED PRACTICE (30-45 minutes)

Materials: Big Idea Posters from Warm-Up, *Champions Music* CD and player, Awards (pp. 177-180), Bookmark (pp. 181-182), Letter Starters (pp. 175-176); writing paper, pen and envelope for each team member and each parent.

Procedure: Team members display Big Idea posters, discuss what they have learned and demonstrate cheers, raps or songs for family members. Team members and parents (or other involved adults) then write personal letters to be sent at a later time. Team members share answers to prayer before the dismissal prayer.

© 2004 Gospel Light. Permission to photocopy granted. *Raising Up Spiritual Champions*

WARM-UP (10-15 minutes)

Preparation: Place poster board and markers on tables large enough for groups of three to four to use. Attach posters to wall.

Materials: *Session 7 Student Page* (pp. 161-162) for each team member, brainstorming posters from Sessions 1-6, masking tape, poster board, markers.

Evaluation and Celebration Preparation!

Procedure: Welcome to our celebration session! During Warm-Up today, check in with me to talk about how you did on your plan from last week. During the time while you are not checking in, look at the posters around the room to help you remember the big ideas of our first six sessions. Then create a Big Idea poster for one session. You can work on a poster by yourself or with a friend or two. The Big Idea posters will have words or drawings to show our guests about the big idea, or main idea, of each session. (Note: If parents will be present, give them Letter Starters page and writing materials. Parents begin writing letters to their children.)

Team members take turns to check in with you and also make one or more Big Idea Posters. Encourage all team members to choose different sessions. (Optional: Brainstorm poster ideas before team members begin work.)

During individual check-ins, first answer one of the questions below about your own week and then ask each team member several of the following questions:

✐ **On a scale of 1 to 10, with 10 being high, how well do you feel you did in completing your plan last week?**

✐ **What was one thing that worked really well?**

- What was the hardest part?

- Which part did you enjoy most?

- What was easy to do? Hard to do?

- What one thing could you do differently that would make you a better disciple?

- Who could you get to help you remember to do that one thing?

As team members work on the posters, ask:

- Which session do you remember best? What makes you remember it?

- For which session did you choose to do a poster? Why?

- What is the best thing you learned?

- What was the funniest thing that happened?

- What could you write or draw to help someone understand that idea well?

Conclusion: When all team members have completed check-in time and have made a poster (either in small groups or individually), you may wish to provide materials for decorating the room for the celebration. See below for ideas. Allow time for team members to decorate the room and prepare snacks and/or drinks.

Preparation for Celebration!

Create an atmosphere of celebration! Inflate balloons, hang crepe-paper streamers and put sports-related decorative items on the walls to give the room a party feel! Tape the finished Big Idea posters to the walls. Invite team members to bring sports jerseys from home to hang on walls.

Don't forget the food! Ahead of time, assign foods to bring (see Session 7 Parent Page) or call families during the week. Team members may prepare snacks and drinks for family members and others who will be participating in the celebration.

© 2004 Gospel Light. Permission to photocopy granted. *Raising Up Spiritual Champions*

POWER-UP (20-35 minutes)

Preparation: Photocopy Buddy Bingo! pages, making one for every family or individual. Clear a large, open area where people can move freely.

Materials: Buddy Bingo! (p. 173), pencils, small prizes for winners.

Procedure: Distribute a Buddy Bingo! page and a pencil to each family or individual. Using the page, each family or person moves around the room, trying to find a person who fits each description on the sheet. A person who fits the description signs the sheet in the appropriate square. Family or individual whose page is completely filled first gets a small prize. (If time is limited, use traditional bingo rules: Winner is the first to get a row across, down or diagonally.)

The goal of this game is for people to enjoy learning about each other and discovering what they have in common. Read names of those on the winner's page along with their descriptions.

CELEBRATORY FOOD AND DRINK!

If you have prepared refreshments for this celebration, serve them after the game. If time is limited, read the answers to the Buddy Bingo! game during refreshment time.

© 2004 Gospel Light. Permission to photocopy granted. *Raising Up Spiritual Champions*

EXTENDED PRACTICE
(30-45 minutes)

1. Big Idea Presentation Time

Materials: Big Idea Posters from Warm-Up, *Champions Music* CD and player, Awards and Bookmark (pp. 177-182).

Two Ways to Present Posters

Formal: Team members may line up in session order, holding their posters in front of a seated audience. As each poster is raised for viewing, team members who worked on that poster describe it and tell about that big idea. Consider videotaping the presentation so that it may be shown to absent family members and to the entire congregation.

Informal: Posters may be taped to walls near the brainstorming posters for each session. Family members move around the room to view the posters. Team members stand near their posters to explain them.

Preparation: Photocopy and complete Awards and Bookmark pages, making one award and bookmark for each team member and an award for each helper. Personalize each team member award, acknowledging actions such as attendance, Bible verse memorization, helpfulness, friendliness, discussion participation, etc.

Procedure: Team members display and talk about posters, about the big ideas and about the things they learned, referring to the brainstorming posters from Sessions 1-6 as needed.

NOTE:
Be sensitive to whether team members are willing to talk during their presentations. Invite volunteers and don't force anyone to talk. The presentation is not meant to embarrass any team member but rather to affirm each one's accomplishments!

Songs. Invite everyone to sing along as team members demonstrate motions that were created and practiced to accompany selected songs. (Optional: If team members have prepared cheers or raps, invite them to demonstrate cheers or raps now.)

Awards. Invite participants to be seated if possible. **Now it's time to honor our team members!** Distribute the prepared award certificates to team members and helpers. As each person comes to receive his or her award, describe that person's accomplishments and applaud heartily!

© 2004 Gospel Light. Permission to photocopy granted. *Raising Up Spiritual Champions*

2. Special Delivery Letters

Materials: Letter Starters (see pp. 175-176); writing paper, pen and envelope for each team member and each adult.

Preparation: Make several copies of Letter Starters pages. Place copies and writing materials on tables. (If placing both adults and team members at the same table, be sure copies of both versions of the Letter Starters are available.)

Procedure: Today, our final assignment is to write some very significant letters. Team members will write letters to themselves and to God. Adults will write letters to their children. The sheets on the tables contain sentence starters. You may choose one of these with which to begin your letter.

These letters are meant to serve as a time of commitment for the team members: They have completed an important step in understanding how to be disciples of **Jesus.** Each team member writes a letter to God and/or him- or herself, using the sentence starters he or she chose. Each adult writes a letter to his or her child, using the sentence starters he or she chose. Each letter is placed in an envelope and appropriately addressed for mailing. (Provide mailing labels for younger children to use if needed.)

Stamp and mail letters at least two weeks later.

Letters for a Lifetime!

These commitment letters are meant to memorialize each team member's discipleship plans in a permanent form. The letters from adults are designed to help adults express love, support for the child's commitments and a reaffirming of the adult's own commitment to help that child become a wholehearted follower of Jesus. These letters will likely become treasured possessions!

Wrap-Up: We've learned that praying for each other helps us grow strong as members of God's team! Who would like to tell about a prayer request we have prayed about? Volunteers tell how God has answered prayer during the course.

Close the celebration with a prayer time, inviting parents and/or team members to pray aloud if desired. End the prayer time by saying, **Thank You, Lord, for helping us learn to grow as a team of followers of Jesus. Please help each of us grow closer to You and closer to each other so that we can become the best team of disciples we can be! In Jesus' name, amen.**

© 2004 Gospel Light. Permission to photocopy granted. *Raising Up Spiritual Champions*

Postseason Play!

Consider planning a fun outing several weeks from now with this group. If possible, pass out flyers for this event as they leave today's celebration. Whether it's meeting to play games at a park or eating together at a fast-food restaurant, simple times of gathering where there is interest and interaction with adults will continue a healthy *t-e-a-m*-building process! (Remember, that's *t*each, *e*ncourage, *a*ssist and *m*entor.) Team members will benefit from continued "alumni" events! See resources on pages 24, 189 and 192 for follow-up ideas.

© 2004 Gospel Light. Permission to photocopy granted. *Raising Up Spiritual Champions*

BUDDY BINGO!

My shirt has a sports team logo on it.	I played T-ball.	I love mud football!	I hate to run.
I watch at least one hour of sports per week.	I love to run.	I have scored a goal in soccer.	I know a good riddle.
I've won a tennis game.	I practice making free throws.	I am wearing tennis shoes.	I have walked in a walk-a-thon for a charity.
I've had perfect attendance during **Raising Up Spiritual Champions.**	I can do a push-up.		
I have coached a sports team.	I know all the words to "Take Me Out to the Ball Game."	I have marched with a band on a football field.	I love golf.
I can say the names of five other people in this room.	I have been to a practice or a game this week.		

© 2004 Gospel Light. Permission to photocopy granted. *Raising Up Spiritual Champions*

Letter Starters

Choose one or more phrases to help you begin your letters to God and to yourself.

I'm really glad that . . .

The best thing I can do now is . . .

One way I want to be different is . . .

Dear God, I feel like . . .

One thing I want to change . . .

Dear God, thank You for . . .

God, please help me to . . .

© 2004 Gospel Light. Permission to photocopy granted. *Raising Up Spiritual Champions*

Letter Starters

Choose one or more of these phrases to help you begin your letter to your child.

I thank God that you . . .

You bring joy to me because . . .

I am glad that you and I can . . .

We will always . . .

I want to help you . . .

Always remember that I . . .

I see you growing in these ways . . .

I am proud of you because . . .

It makes me very glad that . . .

© 2004 Gospel Light. Permission to photocopy granted. *Raising Up Spiritual Champions*

You're a WINNER!

This is to certify that

_____

has attended the

Raising Up Spiritual Champions Discipleship Course.

Congratulations! Keep on following Jesus!

_____
Name of Coach

_____
Date

© 2004 Gospel Light. Permission to photocopy granted. *Raising Up Spiritual Champions*

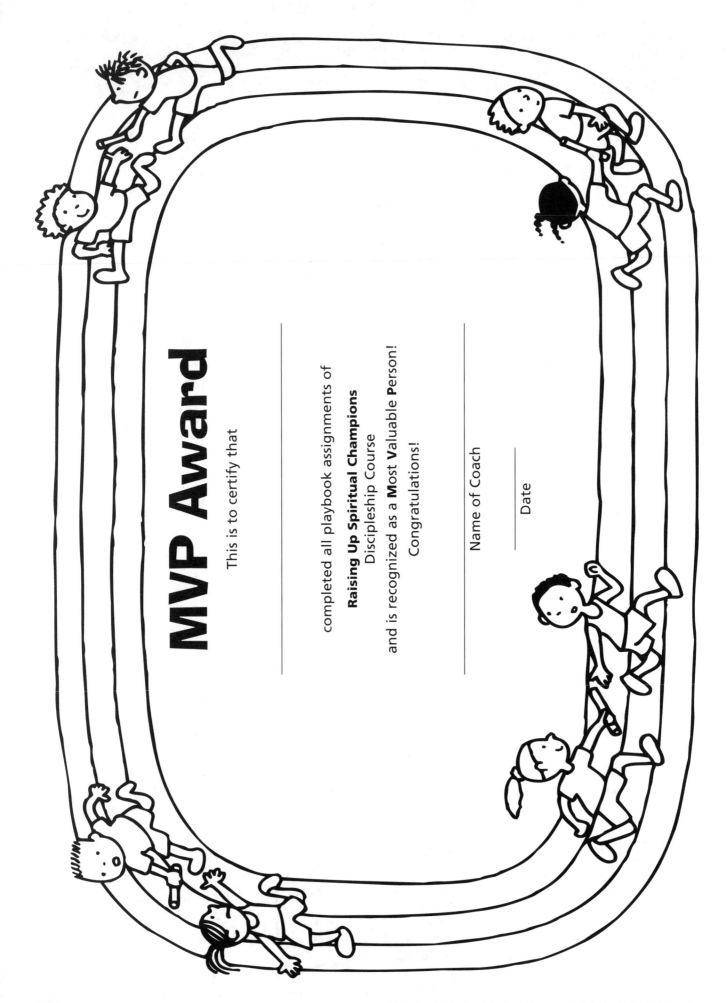

MVP Award

This is to certify that

_____

completed all playbook assignments of
Raising Up Spiritual Champions
Discipleship Course
and is recognized as a **Most Valuable Person!**
Congratulations!

_____
Name of Coach

_____
Date

© 2004 Gospel Light. Permission to photocopy granted. *Raising Up Spiritual Champions*

Most Versatile Person

Award

This is to congratulate and commemorate the efforts of

_____

as a helpful, flexible and appreciated member
of the **Raising Up Spiritual Champions** team.

Thank you for your contribution!

_____
Name of Coach

_____
Date

© 2004 Gospel Light. Permission to photocopy granted. *Raising Up Spiritual Champions*

Champion Award

You're a champion now and forever!

Thanks for joining in at
Raising Up Spiritual Champions

_____
Name of Coach

_____
Date

2 WAY GO

© 2004 Gospel Light. Permission to photocopy granted. _Raising Up Spiritual Champions_

WHERE I CAN GO...

When I'm worried about what I don't have:
Mathew 6:25,33

When I don't know what to say to God:
Romans 8:26

When I need to remember who is in control:
Romans 8:28

When it's hard to like another person:
Romans 15:7

When I'm tempted to worry:
Philippians 4:6-7

When I need to know what to do:
James 1:5

KEEP ON FOLLOWING JESUS!

WHERE I CAN GO...

When I'm worried about what I don't have:
Mathew 6:25,33

When I don't know what to say to God:
Romans 8:26

When I need to remember who is in control:
Romans 8:28

When it's hard to like another person:
Romans 15:7

When I'm tempted to worry:
Philippians 4:6-7

When I need to know what to do:
James 1:5

KEEP ON FOLLOWING JESUS!

WHERE I CAN GO...

When I'm worried about what I don't have:
Mathew 6:25,33

When I don't know what to say to God:
Romans 8:26

When I need to remember who is in control:
Romans 8:28

When it's hard to like another person:
Romans 15:7

When I'm tempted to worry:
Philippians 4:6-7

When I need to know what to do:
James 1:5

KEEP ON FOLLOWING JESUS!

WHERE I CAN GO...

When I'm worried about what I don't have:
Mathew 6:25,33

When I don't know what to say to God:
Romans 8:26

When I need to remember who is in control:
Romans 8:28

When it's hard to like another person:
Romans 15:7

When I'm tempted to worry:
Philippians 4:6-7

When I need to know what to do:
James 1:5

KEEP ON FOLLOWING JESUS!

WHERE I CAN GO...

When I'm worried about what I don't have:
Mathew 6:25,33

When I don't know what to say to God:
Romans 8:26

When I need to remember who is in control:
Romans 8:28

When it's hard to like another person:
Romans 15:7

When I'm tempted to worry:
Philippians 4:6-7

When I need to know what to do:
James 1:5

KEEP ON FOLLOWING JESUS!

WHERE I CAN GO...

When I'm worried about what I don't have:
Mathew 6:25,33

When I don't know what to say to God:
Romans 8:26

When I need to remember who is in control:
Romans 8:28

When it's hard to like another person:
Romans 15:7

When I'm tempted to worry:
Philippians 4:6-7

When I need to know what to do:
James 1:5

KEEP ON FOLLOWING JESUS!

© 2004 Gospel Light. Permission to photocopy granted. *Raising Up Spiritual Champions*

Get your teammates and coaches
to sign their names here!

Get your teammates and coaches
to sign their names here!

Get your teammates and coaches
to sign their names here!

Get your teammates and coaches
to sign their names here!

Get your teammates and coaches
to sign their names here!

Get your teammates and coaches
to sign their names here!

© 2004 Gospel Light. Permission to photocopy granted. *Raising Up Spiritual Champions*

Forms

Look in this section to find helpful forms that you can customize for use in your church. You will find job descriptions, sign-up sheets, publicity flyers and more! Photocopy or print from the CD-ROM the forms you need.

Clip Art

Raising Up
Spiritual Champions

RAISING UP
SPIRITUAL CHAMPIONS

Raising Up
Spiritual Champions

RAISING UP
SPIRITUAL CHAMPIONS

RAISING UP
SPIRITUAL CHAMPIONS

RAISING UP
SPIRITUAL CHAMPIONS

© 2004 Gospel Light. Permission to photocopy granted. *Raising Up Spiritual Champions*

 © 2004 Gospel Light. Permission to photocopy granted. *Raising Up Spiritual Champions*

© 2004 Gospel Light. Permission to photocopy granted. *Raising Up Spiritual Champions*

Daily Devotions

After completing **Raising Up Spiritual Champions**, send one of these Daily Devotions to team members to help them continue developing discipleship habits.

Handy Helpful Habits!

Monday	Acts 1:14—What did the disciples constantly do together? Who could you do this with?
Tuesday	What's a good habit for your head? (See Philippians 4:8.)
Wednesday	Jesus had a habit. What did He often do? (Check out Luke 5:16.) Would this be a good idea for you? Why or why not?
Thursday	Another good habit for you to get into is described in 2 Timothy 3:14-17. What should you keep on doing (or "continue in")?
Friday	Here's another habit: Psalm 1:2. How can you get into this one?
Bonus	Look at Psalm 103:1-5 to find some things to start your habit of prayer with.

Foolproof Ways to Get Wisdom

Monday	Psalm 19:7-11 What will get you from "simple" to "wise"? Memorize one of these verses.
Tuesday	Colossians 2:2-3 Name the person you need to know in order to get wisdom.
Wednesday	James 1:5-6 What are the two things you must do to get wisdom?
Thursday	Proverbs 13:20; 14:6-9 What kinds of people should you hang with? Not hang with? Why?
Friday	Proverbs 3:13-15 What's better than silver, gold and rubies?
Bonus	Daniel 12:3 What will wise people be like when everything is said and done?

Get the Picture!

Monday
Psalm 119:11
What helps you make good decisions?

Tuesday
Psalm 119:18
Who is the psalmist talking to? What's in the law?

Wednesday
Psalm 119:59-61
How can you be a spiritually strong girl or guy?

Thursday
Psalm 119:72-73
How valuable is God's law? Who helps you understand it?

Friday
Psalm 119:102-104
Try praying these words to God!

Bonus
Read at least three sections of Psalm 119. (Each section is marked by a letter of the Hebrew alphabet.)

Confession Is . . .

Monday
In Luke 15:11-32, Jesus told a story about a kid who really blew it. (Read it!) In verses 21-24, what did he confess? And what did his dad say—and do—to him?

Tuesday
In Luke 19:1-10, Jesus met a big-time sinner—up a tree. What did he say to Jesus about his sin? (See verses 8-10.)

Wednesday
Peter did a miserable thing in Mark 14:66-72. What words do you think he might have prayed silently while he did what is reported at the end of verse 72?

Thursday
Read Psalm 51:1-2, written by David. What did this famous Old Testament king ask God to do after he admitted his sin?

Friday
What promises does God make to us if we confess our sins? Read 1 John 1:9!

Bonus
Read Isaiah 1:18 to find another promise to people in need of confession.

© 2004 Gospel Light. Permission to photocopy granted. *Raising Up Spiritual Champions*

SECRET STRENGTH!

MONDAY
In Psalm 51:12, David asks God to "restore to me the joy of your salvation." In Psalm 80, Asaph (a worship leader in Israel) used the word "restore" how many times? (Hint: See verses 3,17,19.)

TUESDAY
In Psalm 80:3, Asaph asks God to "make your face shine upon us." How does your face look when it's shining? How do you feel when your face looks that way? Read Numbers 6:24-26. Why would you want God's face to shine on you?

WEDNESDAY
In Psalm 103, David tells a serious secret about how not to get old! Check out verses 1-5.

THURSDAY
In Psalm 85 (written by the Sons of Korah—more worship leaders!), these guys tell us that when God revives people, another "re" thing happens. What is it? Look at verse 6.

FRIDAY
When we've done all the repenting and God's done the restoring, renewing and reviving, what does Nehemiah 8:10 say will be our strength?

BONUS
Read Nehemiah 8 for a great story!!

THE LAST WORD

MONDAY
Does your nationality matter to God? (Hint: See Galatians 3:28.)

TUESDAY
Should you welcome anyone to church, even barbarians? (Look it up! See Colossians 3:11.)

WEDNESDAY
What does God say you should wear? Wear it every day! See Colossians 3:12.

THURSDAY
When people are different from you, does it bother you? What should you do? (Hint: See Colossians 3:13.)

FRIDAY
In a group of different kinds of people, what holds them together in God? (Try Colossians 3:14.)

BONUS
Read Colossians 3:15-17. What can you do so that these verses describe your church?

© 2004 Gospel Light. Permission to photocopy granted. *Raising Up Spiritual Champions*

Alumni Event!

All graduates of the **Raising Up
Spiritual Champions** discipleship course
are invited to our alumni event!

Where:

When:

What:

Who to contact to RSVP
or for more information:

See you there!

Alumni Event!

All graduates of the **Raising Up
Spiritual Champions** discipleship course
are invited to our alumni event!

Where:

When:

What:

Who to contact to RSVP
or for more information:

See you there!

Alumni Event!

All graduates of the **Raising Up
Spiritual Champions** discipleship course
are invited to our alumni event!

Where:

When:

What:

Who to contact to RSVP
or for more information:

See you there!

Alumni Event!

All graduates of the **Raising Up
Spiritual Champions** discipleship course
are invited to our alumni event!

Where:

When:

What:

Who to contact to RSVP
or for more information:

See you there!

© 2004 Gospel Light. Permission to photocopy granted. *Raising Up Spiritual Champions*

Postseason Team Time!

We've been thinking about you and
praying for you. Let's get together
for some postseason team time!

Where:

When:

To Do What:

Who to contact to RSVP
or for more information:

See you there!

Postseason Team Time!

We've been thinking about you and
praying for you. Let's get together
for some postseason team time!

Where:

When:

To Do What:

Who to contact to RSVP
or for more information:

See you there!

Postseason Team Time!

We've been thinking about you and
praying for you. Let's get together
for some postseason team time!

Where:

When:

To Do What:

Who to contact to RSVP
or for more information:

See you there!

Postseason Team Time!

We've been thinking about you and
praying for you. Let's get together
for some postseason team time!

Where:

When:

To Do What:

Who to contact to RSVP
or for more information:

See you there!

Coordinator

- Schedules **Raising Up Spiritual Champions** program, coordinating dates, times and facilities with the overall church calendar and other church staff as needed

- Recruits, trains and oversees volunteers by providing materials and facilitating communication within the program

Publicity/Event Coordinator

- Plans and carries out publicity to recruit coaches and trainers

- Plans and carries out publicity to encourage team-member participation in the **Raising Up Spiritual Champions** program

- Plans and carries out publicity to team members and families for the Session 8 Family Celebration

Coach

- Prepares and then leads or assists a group of 8 to 12 team members to participate in each session's activities

- Builds relationships with each team member during the **Raising Up Spiritual Champions** program

- Plans one or more follow-up group activities with team members

© 2004 Gospel Light. Permission to photocopy granted. *Raising Up Spiritual Champions*

Curriculum Expert

- Prepares curriculum materials for each session (Sessions, Resource Pages, *Student Pages, Parent Pages*), printing out materials from the CD-ROM or making photocopies from this book

- Optional: Secures binders for *Student Page* Playbooks (see Session 1)

Trainer

- Assists coaches with their responsibilities

- Builds relationships with each team member during the **Raising Up Spiritual Champions** program

- Participates in one or more follow-up group activities with team members

© 2004 Gospel Light. Permission to photocopy granted. *Raising Up Spiritual Champions*

Team Manager

- Prepares the location where sessions take place by setting up room(s) and needed equipment

- Places materials for each activity where they are needed

Secretary/Registrar

- Registers team members and maintains attendance records
- Communicates number of registrations to curriculum expert
- Prepares team rosters for coaches and trainers
- Provides team member contact information as needed to publicity/event coordinator

© 2004 Gospel Light. Permission to photocopy granted. *Raising Up Spiritual Champions*

It's Coming!

Raising Up Spiritual Champions Discipleship Course

Get ready for an eight-week intensive discipleship adventure with a sports theme, designed for children ages 9 to 12! The course includes eight sessions of creative Bible study, meaningful discussion, fun activities and creative homework that involves family members and Bible verses to learn. Participation is limited to children whose parents sign them up and are willing to help with at-home activities.

Time: Place:

To volunteer as a coach, call:

It's Coming!

Raising Up Spiritual Champions Discipleship Course

Get ready for an eight-week intensive discipleship adventure with a sports theme, designed for children ages 9 to 12! The course includes eight sessions of creative Bible study, meaningful discussion, fun activities and creative homework that involves family members and Bible verses to learn. Participation is limited to children whose parents sign them up and are willing to help with at-home activities.

Time: Place:

To volunteer as a coach, call:

Would you like to know the answers to some BIG questions about what it means to follow Jesus?

Then come to **Raising Up Spiritual Champions** that begins on_____.
(date)

It's eight weeks of adventure that you won't want to miss!

Participation is limited to children whose parents sign them up and are willing to help with at-home activities.

Time:

Place:

For more information, call:

Would you like to know the answers to some BIG questions about what it means to follow Jesus?

Then come to **Raising Up Spiritual Champions** that begins on_____.
(date)

It's eight weeks of adventure that you won't want to miss!

Participation is limited to children whose parents sign them up and are willing to help with at-home activities.

Time:

Place:

For more information, call:

© 2004 Gospel Light. Permission to photocopy granted. *Raising Up Spiritual Champions*

Raising Up Spiritual Champions Scope and Sequence

Session	Discipleship Question	Discipleship Action	Bible Memory Verse	Bible Reference	Bible Character
Session 1	What Does It Mean to Be a Disciple?	Discover that being Jesus' disciple means to think and act like Him	"Just as you received Christ Jesus as Lord, continue to live in him, rooted and built up in him, strengthened in the faith as you were taught, and overflowing with thankfulness." Colossians 2:6-7	Mark 1:14-20; John 1:35-49	Jesus calls Andrew and Peter
Session 2	What Is Most Important to Me?	Plan ways to put God first in everyday life	"Seek first his kingdom and his righteousness, and all these things will be given to you as well." Matthew 6:33	Luke 10:38-42	Mary chooses to listen to Jesus
Session 3	How Does Knowing the Truth Make a Difference in My Life?	Discover and practice ways to put God's truth into action	"Show me your ways, O Lord, teach me your paths; guide me in your truth and teach me, for you are God my Savior, and my hope is in you all day long." Psalm 25:4-5	James 1:22-27; 3:1-3	James describes how to know God's wisdom
Session 4	What Happens When I Sin?	Recognize the power of God's forgiveness and plan ways to make a fresh start	"Have mercy on me, O God, according to your unfailing love; according to your great compassion blot out my transgressions. Wash away all my iniquity and cleanse me from my sin." Psalm 51:1-2	John 13:37-38; 18:15-26; 21:1-19	Peter tells about his denial and restoration
Session 5	Where Do I Go for Answers?	Identify ways to trust God in difficult parts of life and under peer pressure	"Stand firm. Let nothing move you. Always give yourself fully to the work of the Lord." 1 Corinthians 15:58	Numbers 13:1-2, 17-33; 14:1-10	Joshua and Caleb trust God when others are fearful
Session 6	Why Do I Need Other Christians?	Practice building up others, so we all can grow as disciples	"Therefore encourage one another and build each other up, just as in fact you are doing." 1 Thessalonians 5:11	Acts 4:36-37; 9:26-30; 11:22-26; 15:36-40	Barnabas encourages others
Session 7	How Do I Plan to Grow as a Disciple? Review and Personal Discipleship Planning	Make and plan ways to carry out a discipleship plan	"Just as you received Christ Jesus as Lord, continue to live in him, rooted and built up in him, strengthened in the faith as you were taught, and overflowing with thankfulness." Colossians 2:6-7		
Session 8	How Did I Do? Evaluation and Celebration	Celebrate individual and team accomplishments in growing as Jesus' disciples	"Just as you received Christ Jesus as Lord, continue to live in him, rooted and built up in him, strengthened in the faith as you were taught, and overflowing with thankfulness." Colossians 2:6-7		

© 2004 Gospel Light. Permission to photocopy granted. *Raising Up Spiritual Champions*

Session Game Plan

Date_____

Aims: 1._____

2. _____

3. _____

Warm-Up (_____minutes)

Coach _____

Trainers _____

Supplies to Collect _____

Comments _____

_____

Power-Up (_____minutes)

Coach _____

Trainers _____

Supplies to Collect _____

Comments _____

_____

Practice (_____minutes)

Coach _____

Trainers _____

Supplies to Collect _____

Comments _____

_____

Rally (_____minutes)

Coach _____

Trainers _____

Supplies to Collect _____

Comments _____

_____

200 • Session Game Plan

© 2004 Gospel Light. Permission to photocopy granted. *Raising Up Spiritual Champions*

Celebrate

Tune in, log on, join the celebration!
God deserves our praise in every situation.

Chorus:
So celebrate, celebrate, celebrate,
Let's clap our hands and sing.
Celebrate, celebrate, celebrate,
Let those praises ring!

God's the same today and yesterday,
    twenty-four-seven;
He loves giving His children good things,
    good gifts from heaven.

Chorus twice

Let's clap our hands and sing!
Jesus is the King!

© 2004 Gospel Light. Permission to photocopy granted. Raising Up Spiritual Champions
Words and Music: Gary Pailer. © 2000 Gospel Light. All rights reserved. Champions Music

Do What It Says

James 1:22-25

There was a brother named James who wrote this letter
Tellin' true believers how to live life better;
And if brother James were here today,
Without a doubt we'd still hear him say:

Do not merely listen to the word, and so deceive yourselves.
Do what it says. (Just do what it says.)

Anyone who listens to the word but does not do what it says
 is like a man who looks at his face in a mirror
 and, after looking at himself, goes away
 and immediately forgets what he looks like.

(So) Do not merely listen to the word,
 and so deceive yourselves.
(But) Do what it says. Do what it says. Do what it says.
Do what it says.

But the man who looks intently into the perfect law that gives
 freedom, and continues to do this, not forgetting what he
 has heard, but doing it—he will be blessed in what he does.
 (Straight Up!)

(So) Do not merely listen to the word,
 and so deceive yourselves.
(But) Do what it says. Do what it says. Do what it says.
Do what it says.

© 2004 Gospel Light. Permission to photocopy granted. Raising Up Spiritual Champions
Music: Darla Plice. © 1996 Gospel Light, Ventura, CA 93006. All rights reserved. Lyrics taken from the Holy Bible, New International Version®. NIV®.
Copyright © 1973, 1978, 1984 by International Bible Society. Used by permission. All rights reserved. Champions Music

Good Habits

Uh-oh! Here comes trouble again!
It's up to me if it will lose or win.
Trouble won't stand a chance, even from the start,
If I've grown faithful habits that
    help to make me smart!

Good habits! Good habits!
Bit by bit by bit, I'm forming good habits!

Most habits we hear about are bad;
    those are the ones that make God sad.
When we trust God every day and do our very best,
We practice praying and helping,
    so we pass that trouble test!

Good habits! Good habits!
Day by day by day, help me form good habits!
Good habits!

Day by day by day,
    day by day by day,
    day by day by day,
Help me form good habits! Good habits!

© 2004 Gospel Light. Permission to photocopy granted. Raising Up Spiritual Champions
Words and Music: Gary Pailer. © 2001 Gospel Light. All rights reserved. Champions Music

I Want to Follow Jesus

In the days of the Bible, came someone called Jesus.
Came to bring the good news, take our sins away.
John said Jesus was God's Son; people followed
    Jesus.
Led them on an adventure, changed all of their lives!

Chorus:
Now I, I want to follow Jesus.
He's the one who takes us on adventures every
    day.
Now I, I want to follow Jesus,
'Cause He's the one who makes us strong
To follow in His ways.

Still He calls us to follow on the great adventure.
Once we hear of God's love, how can we stay away?

Chorus

© 2004 Gospel Light. Permission to photocopy granted. Raising Up Spiritual Champions
Words and Music: Steve Boschetti, Lynnette Pennings, Mary Gross. © 1998 Gospel Light. All rights reserved. Champions Music

Just Ask Him

God will help us when we pray
   (just ask Him, just ask Him);
We all can use help every day
   (just ask Him, just ask Him).

Chorus:
God hears our prayers, so let Him know!
He always cares; He loves us so!

If we ask God's help, He'll help us grow
   (just ask Him, just ask Him);
We'll have more good fruit to show
   (just ask Him, just ask Him).
Love, joy, peace, patience and kindness
   (just ask Him, just ask Him);
Goodness, faithfulness, gentleness, self-control.

Chorus

Love, joy, peace, patience and kindness
   (just ask Him, just ask Him);
Goodness, faithfulness, gentleness, self-control.
Ooh, ooh, ooh (just ask Him);
Ooh, ooh, ooh (just ask Him);
Ooh, ooh, ooh (just ask Him);
Ooh, ooh, ooh.

© 2004 Gospel Light. Permission to photocopy granted. Raising Up Spiritual Champions
Words and Music: Gary Pailer. © 2001 Gospel Light. All rights reserved. Champions Music

Just Like You

Teach me to be like You, Lord Jesus; I want to live like You, Lord Jesus.
Teach me to be like You, Lord Jesus; I want to love like You, Lord Jesus.

Chorus:
I will learn to live my life in ways that please You.
I will learn to do what's right by loving like You do.
I want to be like You.

Teach me to be like You, Lord Jesus; I want to live like You, Lord Jesus.
Teach me to be like You, Lord Jesus; I want to love like You, Lord Jesus.

Chorus

Teach me to be like You. Teach me to be like You.
Teach me to be like You, Lord Jesus.

© 2004 Gospel Light. Permission to photocopy granted. Raising Up Spiritual Champions
Words and Music: Gary Pailer. © 2001 Gospel Light. All rights reserved. Champions Music

Moth and Rust

Matthew 6:19-21,24

Do not store up for yourselves treasures on earth,
    where moth and rust destroy,
    and where thieves break in and steal.
But store up for yourselves treasures in heaven,
    where moth and rust do not destroy,
    and where thieves do not break in and steal.

For where your treasure is, for where your treasure is,
    for where your treasure is, there your heart will be also,
    there your heart will be also.

No one can serve two masters.
You cannot serve both God and Money.
No one can serve two masters.
You cannot serve both God and Money.
Either he will hate the one and love the other,
    or he will be devoted to the one and despise the other.

For where your treasure is, for where your treasure is,
    for where your treasure is, there your heart will be also,
    there your heart will be also.

© 2004 Gospel Light. Permission to photocopy granted. Raising Up Spiritual Champions
Music: Marc and Judy Roth. © 1997 Gospel Light, Ventura, CA 93006. All rights reserved. Lyrics taken from the Holy Bible, New International
Version®. NIV®. Copyright © 1973, 1978, 1984 by International Bible Society. Used by permission. All rights reserved. Champions Music

Psalm 51:1-4,10-12

Chorus:

Create in me a pure heart, O God.
Create in me a pure heart, O God.
Create in me a pure heart, O God,
   and renew a steadfast spirit within me.
Do not cast me from your presence
   or take your Holy Spirit from me.
Restore to me the joy of your salvation
   and grant me a willing spirit, to sustain me.

Have mercy on me, O God,
   according to your unfailing love;
According to your great compassion
   blot out my transgressions.

Create in me a pure heart, O God.
Create in me a pure heart, O God.

Wash away all my iniquity and cleanse me from my sin,
For I know my transgressions
   and my sin is always before me.

Create in me a pure heart, O God.
Create in me a pure heart, O God.

Against you, you only, have I sinned
   and done what is evil in your sight
So that you are proved right when you speak and justified
   when you judge.

Chorus

© 2004 Gospel Light. Permission to photocopy granted. Raising Up Spiritual Champions
Music: Mary Gross. © 1996 Gospel Light, Ventura, CA 93006. All rights reserved. Lyrics taken from the Holy Bible, New International Version®. NIV®.
Copyright © 1973, 1978, 1984 by International Bible Society. Used by permission. All rights reserved. Champions Music

Psalm 119:10-12

I seek You with all my heart;
Do not let me stray from Your commands.
I have hidden Your word in my heart
That I might not sin against You.

Praise be to You, O Lord; teach me Your decrees.
Praise be to You, O Lord; teach me Your decrees.

© 2004 Gospel Light. Permission to photocopy granted. Raising Up Spiritual Champions
Music: Mary Gross. © 1998 Gospel Light, Ventura, CA 93006. All rights reserved. Lyrics taken from the Holy Bible, New International Version®. NIV®.
Copyright © 1973, 1978, 1984 by International Bible Society. Used by permission. All rights reserved. Champions Music

Teamwork

All God's people, time to join in.
Come together, let the games begin!
God has called us to be His team,
So let's work together with love extreme.

Chorus:
Teamwork! Pray for one another.
Teamwork! Cheer for each other.
It's our God we're livin' for, and together, everyone
    accomplishes more.
We're on God's team with love extreme,
And together, everyone accomplishes more!

Encourage each other with the love He gives—
Show the world that our Savior lives.
God has called us to be His team,
So let's work together with love extreme.

Teamwork! Pray for one another.
Teamwork! Cheer for each other.
It's our God we're livin' for, and together, everyone
    accomplishes more.

T-E-A-M—What does it mean?
God has called us to be His team.
Four little letters—What do they stand for?
Together everyone accomplishes more!

Chorus

© 2004 Gospel Light. Permission to photocopy granted. Raising Up Spiritual Champions
By Cathy Spurr. © 2004 Parbar Music. Used by permission. Champions Music

Trust in the Lord

Proverbs 3:5-6

Trust in the Lord with all your heart
And lean not on your own understanding;
In all your ways acknowledge Him,
And He will make your paths straight.

Chorus:
Trust in the Lord. (Trust in the Lord.)
He's like solid ground. (Trust in the Lord.)
Trust in the Lord. (Trust in the Lord.)
He will never (He will never) let (never let) you
**   down!**

© 2004 Gospel Light. Permission to photocopy granted. Raising Up Spiritual Champions
Words and Music: Gary Pailer. © 2003 Gospel Light. All rights reserved. Champions Music

You Promised

You help me to know (every day);
You help me to grow (in every way);
You help me to see (what to do);
You help me to be more like You.

Chorus:
You promised (Lord, I love You),
You promised (You always come through),
You promised; Your word is true.
You promised (Lord, I love You),
You promised (You always come through),
You promised; I can count on You.

Please help me to care (lend a hand);
Please help me to share (all I can);
Please help me to give (like You give);
Please help me to live more like You.

Chorus

I can count on You. (You promised!)
I can count on You.

© 2004 Gospel Light. Permission to photocopy granted. Raising Up Spiritual Champions
Words and Music: Gary Pailer. © 2001 Gospel Light. All rights reserved. Champions Music

Supply List

Provide these supplies for every session.

- ❏ Bible for each team member
- ❏ Butcher paper
- ❏ CD player
- ❏ Construction paper
- ❏ Markers
- ❏ Masking tape
- ❏ *Champions Music* CD
- ❏ Paper
- ❏ *Parent Pages*
- ❏ Pencils
- ❏ Scissors
- ❏ *Student Pages*

Session 1
- ❏ Three copies of "Let Me Tell You!" (pp. 61-64)
- ❏ Strategy Stations (pp. 65-66)

For every eight team members:
- ❏ Trash can or sturdy basket
- ❏ Eight index cards
- ❏ Foam ball

Session 2
- ❏ 10-15 household items in a bag

For every four to eight team members:
- ❏ Baseball bat

Session 3
- ❏ What's My Question? (pp. 91-92)
- ❏ A variety of items that give a reflection (spoon, shiny bowl, piece of aluminum foil, etc.), including a hand mirror
- ❏ Several dot stickers

Session 4
- ❏ Case Study Cards (p. 105)
- ❏ Peter's Interview Cards (pp. 107-108)
- ❏ The Rest of the Story Cards (p. 106)
- ❏ Soft ball
- ❏ Envelope

For every four to five students:
- ❏ Inflated balloon

Supply List

Session 5

- ❑ "Mission: Possible?" (pp. 121-123)

- ❑ What Happened Next? Cards (p. 124)

- ❑ Distraction! Cards (p. 125)

- ❑ Verse Cards (p. 126)

- ❑ Amazing Itty-Bitty Bible Journal (pp. 127-128)

For every six to eight team members:

- ❑ Rope, 3-6 feet (.9-1.8 m) long

- ❑ Four large plastic garbage bags

- ❑ Spy costumes and props

- ❑ Obstacle-course items (broom, chair, table, hula hoop, yarn, etc.)

Session 6

- ❑ Four copies of "Without You!" (pp. 141-143)

- ❑ Several Bible concordances (may be included in Bibles)

- ❑ Index cards

Session 7

- ❑ Say What? (pp. 157-159)

- ❑ Index cards

- ❑ Lunch bags

- ❑ Station items (chenille wire, play dough or clay, audiocassette recorder and blank cassette or handheld video recorder and videocassette)

- ❑ Materials for personal reminders (crayons, nature items, glue, card stock, yarn or embroidery floss, river stones, glitter glue, beads)

Session 8

- ❑ Buddy Bingo! (p. 173)

- ❑ Awards (pp. 177-180)

- ❑ Bookmark (pp. 181-182)

- ❑ Letter Starters (pp. 175-176)

- ❑ Poster board

- ❑ Small prizes

For each team member and each parent:

- ❑ Writing paper

- ❑ Pen

- ❑ Envelope

© 2004 Gospel Light. Permission to photocopy granted. *Raising Up Spiritual Champions*

Team Attendance

Names	Sessions							
	1	2	3	4	5	6	7	8

© 2004 Gospel Light. Permission to photocopy granted. *Raising Up Spiritual Champions*

Team Roster

Name _____

Address _____

Home Phone _____ Cellular Phone _____

E-Mail Address _____

Parent's Name(s) _____

Name _____

Address _____

Home Phone _____ Cellular Phone _____

E-Mail Address _____

Parent's Name(s) _____

Name _____

Address _____

Home Phone _____ Cellular Phone _____

E-Mail Address _____

Parent's Name(s) _____

Name _____

Address _____

Home Phone _____ Cellular Phone _____

E-Mail Address _____

Parent's Name(s) _____

 © 2004 Gospel Light. Permission to photocopy granted. *Raising Up Spiritual Champions*

Volunteer Sign-Up

I'd like to join the *Raising Up Spiritual Champions* Team! Please contact me with more information!

Name _____

Address _____

Phone Number _____ Cellular Phone _____

E-Mail Address _____

Best Time to Reach Me _____

Name _____

Address _____

Phone Number _____ Cellular Phone _____

E-Mail Address _____

Best Time to Reach Me _____

Name _____

Address _____

Phone Number _____ Cellular Phone _____

E-Mail Address _____

Best Time to Reach Me _____

Name _____

Address _____

Phone Number _____ Cellular Phone _____

E-Mail Address _____

Best Time to Reach Me _____

Using the CD-ROM

Contained on the *Raising Up Spiritual Champions* CD-ROM are two file formats:
1. **JPG**—JPG files are clip-art images that **must be imported** into your word-processing or page-layout application.
2. **PDF**—PDF files are awards, certificates, etc. They can be printed as is via Adobe Acrobat Reader, or saved as EPS files and imported into most slide-show, word-processing and page-layout applications.

JPG Instructions

Important Notes: You cannot open these files directly. These files may be too large for certain applications to be able to show you a preview.

Here's what to do:

1. Open the application you wish to use.
2. Open an existing document or create a new document.
3. Paste (import) the JPG into the document.
4. Enlarge or reduce the image according to your needs. (For specific instructions on how to use the image within your application, refer to your application manual.)

PDF Instructions

Important Notes: PDF files can be opened and printed by using Adobe Acrobat Reader software. PDF files on this CD-ROM cannot be modified via Adobe Acrobat Reader. You can download the most recent version of Acrobat Reader for free from the Adobe website, http://www.adobe.com/products/acrobat/read step2.html.

A PDF file cannot be inserted into most slide-show or word-processing applications. However, the PDF file can be saved as an EPS file following the few simple steps listed below in "Adapting PDF Files." The EPS file you create can be inserted as a picture into most slide-show and word-processing applications.

Adapting PDF Files

Important Note: The EPS file you create can be inserted as a picture file into most slide-show and word-processing applications.

Here's what to do:

1. Open the PDF file using Adobe Acrobat Reader.
2. Go to the FILE menu on the toolbar. Select PAGE SETUP. Make sure page orientation matches the orientation of the image.
3. Go to the FILE menu on the toolbar. Select PRINT (this will bring up the PRINT dialog box).
   a. Change the Destination to FILE.
   b. Change General to SAVE AS FILE.
   c. Change Format to EPS STANDARD PREVIEW.
   d. Choose PostScript Level: LEVEL 2 AND 3.
   e. Choose Data Format: ASCII.
   f. No change needs to be made to Printer selection.
4. Select SAVE.
5. Save file to desired location.

Tips for Using EPS files in Microsoft® PowerPoint® and Microsoft® Word

- When inserting an EPS file into Microsoft Word as a picture file, be sure to check the FLOAT OVER TEXT box when opening the EPS file. Please refer to your Microsoft Word manual for additional help.

© 2004 Gospel Light. Permission to photocopy granted. *Raising Up Spiritual Champions*

- EPS files cannot be directly edited in Microsoft PowerPoint or Microsoft Word. However, you can easily place a TEXT BOX over the image to personalize the document. Be sure to format the TEXT BOX with NO FILL and NO LINE. Please refer to your Microsoft Word manual for additional help.
- EPS files are generally larger than jpeg files, will use more memory and usually take longer to print.
- In order to edit the EPS file or save as a jpeg, you will need a page-layout application such as Adobe PhotoShop, Adobe® Illustrator, Quark, etc.

Problems?

If you have any problems that you can't solve by reading the manual that came with your word-processing or page-layout application, please call the number for the technical support department printed in your software manual. (Sorry, but Gospel Light cannot provide software support.)

© 2004 Gospel Light. Permission to photocopy granted. *Raising Up Spiritual Champions*

Building Tomorrow's Church Begins with *Today's* Children

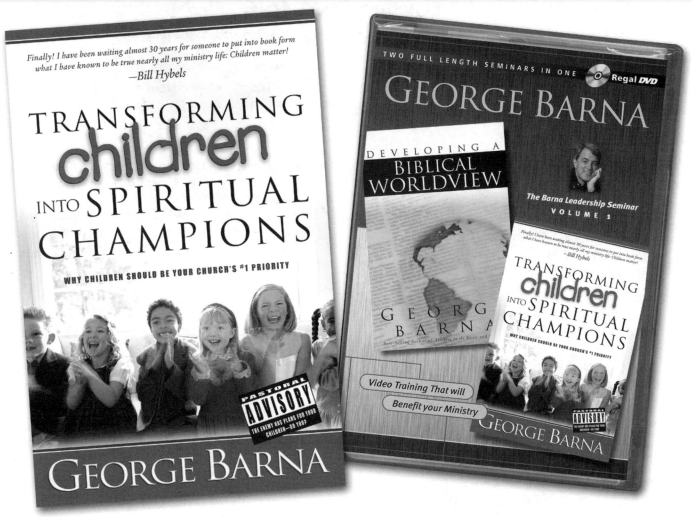

Transforming Children into Spiritual Champions • Why Children Should Be Your Church's #1 Priority
George Barna • Hardcover • ISBN 08307.32934 • DVD • UPC 607135.008521

Church leaders everywhere are discovering George Barna's jolting new statistics for why children need to be your number one priority. Most churches focus on teens and adults instead of young children—but a child's moral development is set by the age of nine!

Make Your Sunday School a Place of Spiritual Training!

Barna gives you real-world solutions on equipping parents to continue their children's spiritual education at home, as well as guidance on reinforcing the biblical effectiveness of your church's Sunday School. The result is a doubly powerful message that turns children into spiritual champions!

Pick Up a Copy at Your Favorite Christian Bookstore!

Visit **www.regalbooks.com** to join **Regal's FREE e-newsletter.** You'll get useful **excerpts from our newest releases** and **special access to online chats with your favorite authors.** Sign up today!

Regal
God's Word for Your World™
www.regalbooks.com

THE ALL-PURPOSE CHILDREN'S MINISTRY SOLUTION!

For Grades 1 to 6

KidsTime is perfect for those times of the week when teachers need a **flexible, easy-to-use program**, or when there aren't enough teachers and children of different ages need to be combined into one group. These "year in a box" programs are an unbeatable value!

Use **KidsTime** for: Any number of kids • Any number of teachers • Limited budgets • Second hour on Sunday • Children's church • Midweek programs • Evening programs • Whenever you have a group of kids!

52-Lesson Kit
Grades 1 to 6
Reproducible
ISBN 08307.23455

Now teachers can make sure their kids get **God's Big Picture**—not just bits and pieces. With **KidsTime: God's Big Picture**, teachers can show them how the whole Bible fits together, the way God meant it. This course is packed with fun activities for kids and brings Scripture into focus as a beautiful portrait of God's love for His people and His interaction with them.

52-Lesson Kit
Grades 1 to 6
Reproducible
ISBN 08307.25415

KidsTime: God's People Celebrate gives kids the big picture of worship as they celebrate His gifts to us. Each lesson includes Bible stories, worship, music, games, art, puzzles and object talks. Includes Old Testament holiday celebrations, church calendar and seasonal holidays.

52-Lesson Kit
Grades 1 to 6
Reproducible
ISBN 08307.25792

KidsTime: God's Kids Grow Kit gives teachers a whole year's worth of fun-filled lessons that help kids explore the **fruit of the Spirit** through art, songs, games, Bible stories, service projects and more! Plus, kids can discover real-life stories of how Christians have shown the fruit of the Spirit. It's a great way to help kids grow the fruit of the Spirit in their own lives.

Gospel Light
God's Word for a Kid's World!™
www.gospellight.com

Available at your Gospel Light supplier or by calling 1-800-4-GOSPEL.

Gospel Light Is God's Word for a Kid's World

At Gospel Light, we remember what it's like to see the world through a child's eyes. That's why our Sunday School curriculum is designed to **reach kids right where they are**. We help them learn about God and His Word through **hands-on activities** that engage their intense curiosity and openness to learning new things.

For **over 70 years**—since Dr. Henrietta Mears wrote the first lesson in 1933—Gospel Light has equipped teachers with the best tools for reaching children with God's love.

Find out for yourself why Gospel Light Sunday School curriculum is God's Word for a kid's world!

ISBN 08307.26578

We Take Kids Through the Bible Four Times by the Time They Leave Grade Six

For **FREE curriculum samples**, to order a starter pack, or to receive more information, contact your Gospel Light supplier or call **1-800-4-GOSPEL**.

Gospel Light
God's Word for a Kid's World!™
www.gospellight.com

ㄥ